Harold Country

Rathfar

Joe Curtis

Second Edition in colour 2019

First Return Press
11 Park Avenue
Rathfarnham
Dublin 16

Distributed by Amazon

ISBN: 9781091526600

Cover Photograph: Loreto Abbey, courtesy of Loreto Archives.

Contents

Acknowledgements

Thanks to the excellent staff of the various official sources of knowledge, including the National Library, National Archives, Irish Architectural Archive, Valuation Office, Trinity College Dublin, Dublin City Library & Archives, South Dublin Libraries (especially the Local Studies section), Representative Church Body Library (RCB), Ballyroan Library, Office of Public Works, Rathfarnham Castle, Pearse Museum, Military Archives, and to the many people who allowed me visit their premises and take photographs. A special thanks is due to the following:

Aine McHugh (Loreto Archives), Damien Burke (Jesuit Archives), Barbara O'Neill (Castle Golf Club), Michael Healy (Rathfarnham Golf Club), Joy Morrissey (Grange Golf Club), Edmondstown Golf Club, Canon Adrianne Galligan (Rathfarnham Anglican Church), Rev Horace McKinley & Pamela McKinley (Whitechurch Anglican Church), Reg Richards (Whitechurch Parish), Fr Martin Cosgrove (Church of the Annunciation, Sr Helen Cunningham (Sisters of Charity), Sally Gibbs (St Columba's College), Bernie Keogh (Three Rock Rovers Hockey Club), Ben Malone & Ray Keogh (Rathfarnham Scouts), Dr Mary Clark (Dublin City Archivist), Enda Leaney (Dublin City Library & Archives), Teresa Whitington (Central Catholic Library), Noel Collins (Office of Public Works), Brian Prendergast (Augustinian Archives), Ann Moloney (Saplings School), David Nolan (Rockbrook Park School), Catherine Keane (Fingal Local Studies), Anna Jennings (Scoil Naomh Padraig), Noelle Dowling (Diocesan Archives), Michael Keyes (South Dublin Libraries), Shane Ryan (South Dublin Libraries), Marianne Cosgrave (Sisters of Mercy Archives), Aoife Torpey (Kilmainham Gaol Museum), Brian Crowley (Kilmainham Gaol Museum), Joe Mac Suibhne (Gaelcholaiste an Phiarsaigh), Stephen Walsh (J.C. Walsh & Sons Ltd), Alan Phelan (Erasmus Smith Schools Archives at The High School, Rathgar), Roy Pearson (Quaker Archives), St Lukes Hospital, Daphne Metcalfe (Church of Ireland Theological Institute), Sr Mary Egan (Little Company of Mary), Liam O'Connor (Mount Carmel Community Hospital), Laura Magnier (Carmelite Library & Archives).

Veteran local historian, Seamus Kelly, was very generous in sharing photos and dispensing knowledge.

All sources of photos are acknowledged individually, unless from the author's own collection.

Brief Background

After the Cromwellian war in Ireland, Oliver Cromwell ordered the Civil Survey to be undertaken in 1654-1656, to value the land of the entire country, in order to decide which Catholic lands were to be taken from the Irish and given to his Protestant soldiers and "adventurers" (financial backers), as payment in lieu of their wages and investments. In addition, it was decided to carry out a more-meaningful measured survey of the country in 1656- 1658, under the control of William Petty. This survey became known as the "Down Survey", because the land measurements were "written down" following the calculations of the soldiers who carried out the hard graft with the aid of "chains" – long iron chains were stretched out in the fields, and land features measured from this baseline. As a result of this unique and momentous task, every townland in Ireland was assessed, listing the major landowners as either Papists or Protestants, and whether the land was unprofitable or usable.

Rathfarnham is a large area in the foothills of the Dublin Mountains, partly in the Barony of Newcastle & Uppercross, and partly in the Barony of Rathdown, and in the Down Survey comprised many townlands. The townland of Rathfarnham stretched from the River Dodder, south as far as present-day Sarah Curran Avenue, bounded by Willbrook Road on the west, and Churchtown on the east. Adam Loftus, Lord Viscount of Ely, a Protestant, was the only owner listed in 1641 and 1670, while in the 1659 Census, there were 16 English and 23 Irish residing in the townland.

The townland of Harold's Grange (actually listed as Kilmakeoge) comprised present-day St Enda's Park, Hermitage housing estate, the north part of Grange Golf Club, and Marlay Grange House (abutting Taylors Lane). John Harrold was the owner in 1641, and Sir Maurice Eustace in 1670, both Protestants. In the 1659 Census, there were 16 English and 5 Irish residents.

The townland of Taylor's Grange (also known as Grange) comprised the east half of present-day Marlay Park, stretching south beyond the M50 Motorway to encompass St Columba's College, and was owned by the Protestant Church.

The townland of Kilmashogue was immediately to the west of Taylor's Grange, taking in the west half of present-day Marlay Park, and the south part of Grange Golf Club. John Harrold was the owner in 1641, and Sir Maurice Eustace in 1670. The 1659 Census listed 19 English and 3 Irish residents. However, the townland of Clarkstown (also called Great Newtowne), owned by Adam Loftus, was sandwiched between the two sections of the golf club. Nowadays Clarkstown is known as Whitechurch.

The townlands of Edmondstown, Ballyboden, Willbrook, Old Orchard, and Butterfield, completed the landscape back north to the River Dodder, mostly owned by the Loftus family. Interestingly, Willbrook was also known as Milltowne, which was very appropriate because of the number of mills which are noted on later maps, and here the Irish outnumbered the English by 14 to 5.

It can be seen from the foregoing that the Loftus family were the biggest landowners in the locality, with John Harrold the next in importance. Harrold may also have been a tenant of Loftus, and therefore a more prominent local figure. Certainly, the name is remembered in Harold's Grange Road, and also in a small house called Harold's Grange which once stood on the site of the present Taylors Three Rock pub.

Harold is reputed to be a Danish family, who were based in the foothills of the Dublin Mountains for hundreds of years before the Down Survey of the 17th century. The famous village of Harold's Cross, a few miles north of Rathfarnham, is reputed to have got its name from a cross or boundary stone, marking the boundary of the Archbishop's land, as a warning to the Harold family not to encroach any further. Ball, in his history of County Dublin, says that Sir John Harold, Knight, was mentioned in 1247, and Sir Geoffrey Harold, Knight, later that century, followed by

Peter Harold at the beginning of the 14th century. Skipping forward to the beginning of the 18th century, the lands of Harold's Grange were in the hands of Thomas Taylor, and then one of his sons, Thomas, who became Lord Mayor of Dublin. After the death of Thomas, the lands were acquired by David La Touche.

Rathfarnham still has many placenames incorporating the word "Grange". The word once denoted a large farm or demesne, since this was all agricultural land a long time ago.

After Adam Loftus completed his castle in 1585, the present village of Rathfarnham developed to supply the needs of the castle, although it is reputed that a very basic village was already in existence when Loftus arrived. At any rate, no buildings from that period survive, and even today, only a handful of 18th and 19th century buildings are in existence. Most of the east side of the Main Street has been rebuilt in recent decades, and a strip of the original castle grounds was developed as medium-rise apartments and some offices (Rathfarnham Gate in 1996 -98), and a By-Pass, while traffic was restricted to a north-south direction in the original village.

Horse-drawn trams with open-topped upper decks, running on tracks, were introduced to Dublin in 1872, and reached Rathfarnham towards the end of that decade. The symbol for this route was the green Maltese Cross, and later the number 16, and the terminus was on Main Street. The system was electrified in the late 1890's. From the mid 1920's, buses began to appear and competed with the trams, until the last tram to Rathfarnham in 1939.

Richard Frizell's 1779 map of Rathfarnham, with the castle at the bottom, the old church in the centre, the old paper mill and waterwheel to left of church, and Ashfield House at the top. (Courtesy of National Library of Ireland).

Rathfarnham Castle

The word "rath" is included in three neighbouring suburbs on the south side of Dublin – Rathmines, Rathgar, and Rathfarnham. "Rath" denoted an earthen fort in bygone days.

In 1583, Adam Loftus, originally from Yorkshire, England, and who was both Lord Chancellor of Ireland and Archbishop of Dublin at the time, was granted the lands in the Rathfarnham area of Dublin, and immediately built a fortified house with four corner defensive towers (which was later called a castle), which is still standing today, although modified on many occasions over the centuries, including adding a bow window on the east elevation, and a kitchen extension at the south-west corner, both in the 18th century. There is no record of any previous "rath" or building on this site.

In 1723, the Duke of Wharton, who had inherited the castle through his mother, Lucy Loftus, sold the castle to William Connolly (Speaker Connolly) of Castletown, County Kildare, who in turn, leased it to various tenants.

In 1769, Henry Loftus was in occupation, as the Earl of Ely, and he is credited with building (assumed sometime in the early 1770's) the impressive Roman triumphal arch (actually a pair of gatehouses) on the present Dodder Park Road, although the original Gothic archway castle entrance off Main Street was still retained. He also had a townhouse called Ely House, in Ely Place, beside Merrion Square, which these days is occupied by the Knights of St Columbanus. However, in the 1780's, he abandoned the castle, and it was not until 1850, that the castle was bought by Lord Chief Justice Blackburne.

Bailey & Gibson, developers, bought the castle on 290 acres in 1912, with the intention of building a housing estate and a golf course. They sold the castle itself and some land to the

Jesuits in 1913. The Castle golf club was opened in 1913. Housing estates had to wait until two World Wars were finished.

In 1913, the Jesuits (Society of Jesus) bought the castle from Bailey & Gibson, builders, as a House of Studies for Junior Jesuits attending UCD in Earlsfort Terrace. In the early years, there were on average 26 residents — 10 priests, who did "Missions" around the country, 14 Juniors, and 2 Brothers. The Jesuits employed farm and house workers, assisted by the two Brothers.

The Retreat House wing, attached to the north-west side of the castle, was built in 1922, which had residential accommodation for working men on weekend "Retreats", and for schoolboy Retreats during the week. A chapel and refectory (diningroom) were added to the Retreat House in 1926, in a three storey projection at the south-west corner of this block, and in 1928, inspiring Harry Clarke stained-glass windows were installed in the chapel (referred to as the Domestic Chapel). The ground floor of this Retreat House comprised two barrel-vaulted rooms of an outdoor store beside the castle, nicknamed Cromwell's Fort, and probably nearly as old as the castle — a photograph before the wing was built by the Jesuits shows a slated steeply pitched roof with central bell-cote. Another big wing was added in 1925 to the south-west corner of the castle, for the Junior priests, in addition to a single-storey community refectory (behind the present café).

The Dublin United Tramway Company (DUTC) had regular Retreats in Rathfarnham Castle. They built the grotto of Our Lady of Lourdes in the grounds, and the official blessing in 1925 was captured by British Pathe News.

The Juniorate closed in 1975, and the Retreat House closed in 1986. The castle was declared a National Monument in 1986, and the Office of Public Works (OPW) bought the Castle in 1987, while Dublin County Council bought the grounds for a public park, including the castle outbuildings nearest the carpark. The gothic archway, which was the original castle entrance from Main Street, was demolished shortly afterwards.

The Harry Clarke stained glass windows (1928) from the retreat house chapel were dismantled, and donated to two different organisations: one three-light window went to the Hospice in Harold's Cross, and six panels to the newly rebuilt (following a fire in 1983) Catholic church in Tullamore, County Offaly. Four decorative panels from the other chapel in the Castle itself (the former ballroom), presumably much earlier work of Harry Clarke, went to Temple Street Childrens Hospital in Dublin. The panels were installed in the Sisters of Charity Convent near the hospital. These four small panels depict religious symbols as opposed to religious figures/saints. One panel is wall-mounted (backlit) on a staircase, another wall-mounted in a corridor, another in a window in the nuns private chapel, and the last is wall mounted in the public St Anthony's Shrine in the former Nurses Home. The windows of the chapel inside the childrens hospital contain only ordinary clear glass.

In the late 1980's, the OPW demolished the two 1920's wings, but thankfully had the good sense to retain the ancient ground floor of the former Retreat House, with its vaulted brick roof, which is currently being restored by South Dublin County Council, together with the former stables.

The castle is still undergoing restoration by the OPW, but two floors are open to the public, where beautiful plasterwork, murals, and joinery can be seen, although the building lacks an impressive staircase. There is a nice model of Rathfarnham Village on display, based on the 1837 Ordnance Survey map. A big hoard of 16th century artifacts was found during excavations for a new lift pit, and is now in the care of the National Museum.

The Ely Arch, which contains two lodges, is still on Lower Dodder Road, having been restored by South Dublin County Council a few years ago. The lodges were occupied up until about 1977, and have been vacant ever since. Each lodge has a small ground floor room, with a corner fireplace, with a steep stair/ladder leading to a small first floor room. The chimney flues are concealed in the corner urns on the roof.

Many lay people have fond memories of Fr John Sullivan (1861-1933), who was a convert to Catholicism, and was the son of Sir Edward Sullivan, Lord Chancellor of Ireland, 1883-1885. Fr John was the Rector of Rathfarnham Castle from 1919 to 1924, and is on the way to being canonised a Saint, now with the title Blessed John Sullivan.

Another interesting Jesuit priest was Fr William O'Leary, who built a seismograph in the castle in 1915, which recorded the earthquake in Japan in 1923.

Until 1979, there was a charming folly, dating from the castle era, known as the Gazebo, near the 10th green on the Castle Golf course, being a two-storey circular masonry building, with a separate colonnade around the base. A circular pigeon house still stands in a back garden at the west end of Crannagh Road.

Fr William O'Leary with his seismograph in Rathfarnham Castle in 1915.
(Courtesy of Jesuit Archives)

Rathfarnham Castle, with north Retreat House. (Courtesy of Jesuit Archives).

Rathfarnham Castle, with south wing House of Studies. (Courtesy of Jesuit Archives).

Rathfarnham Castle, with Retreat House on right, and House of Studies on left. (Courtesy of Jesuit Archives).

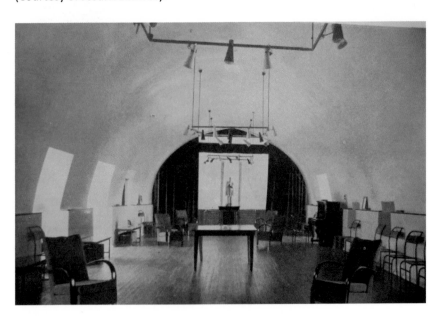

Ground floor of Retreat House wing, Rathfarnham Castle, was nick-named "Cromwell's Fort". Currently being restored. (Courtesy of Jesuit Archives).

Blessed John Sullivan was Rector of Rathfarnham Castle, 1919-1924.
(Courtesy of Jesuit Archives)

Chapel in Retreat House wing of Rathfarnham Castle, contained Harry Clarke
stained-glass windows made in 1928. (Courtesy of Jesuit Archives).

Harry Clarke stained glass window was in the priest's chapel inside Rathfarnham Castle, which was formerly the ballroom. Now in Temple Street Convent.

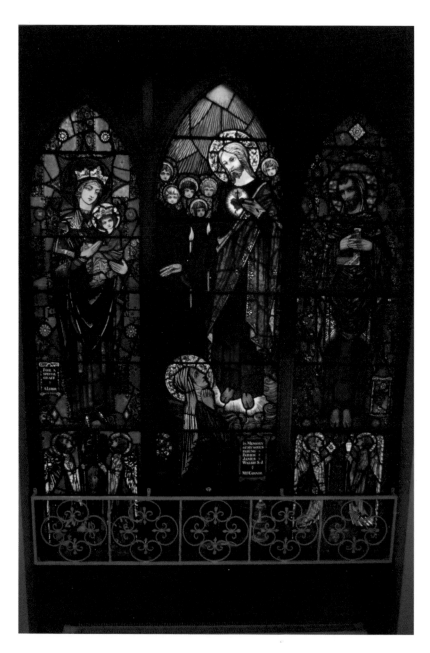

1928 Harry Clarke stained-glass window from the Retreat House wing of Rathfarnham Castle is now in the Hospice, Harold's Cross, on the service staircase behind the lift in the original 1888 building.

Loreto Abbey & Beaufort

Loreto Abbey Boarding School

The Institute of the Blessed Virgin Mary was founded by Mary Ward (from Yorkshire in England), at the beginning of the 17th century, in St. Omer, France, and she also started the Bar Convent in York, in 1686. The Irish branch of the IBVM is known as the Loreto Nuns, and was started in 1821 by Mother Teresa Ball, also known as Frances Ball. Frances was born in 1794 in 43, Eccles Street (now No. 63), to a wealthy Dublin Catholic family, and her father John Ball (a Catholic convert) was a silk manufacturer. Frances was sent to school at the age of nine to St. Mary's Convent, Mickelgate Bar, York, as was the practice with many wealthy Catholic families of the day.

Dr. Daniel Murray (later Archbishop) bought Rathfarnham House with forty acres in 1821, for £2,300, (paid by Anna Maria O'Brien - nee Ball), in preparation for the founding of the Institute of the Blessed Virgin Mary in Ireland. On 8th August 1821, Mother Teresa arrived in Ireland from York, in company with Sr. Baptist (Anne Therry of Cork), and Sr. Ignatia (Eleanor Arthur of Limerick), and took up temporary residence for eight months with the newly founded Sisters of Charity in Stanhope Street, while Rathfarnham House was being repaired. However, the three nuns were anxious to embark on educating young girls, and so they rented a small house adjoining the Poor Clare Convent in Harold's Cross for six months, from 5th May 1822 to 3rd November 1822, and here they opened the first school of the Loreto nuns in Ireland. There is no information on the exact house which was acquired, but it was probably the present No. 87 Harold's Cross Road, which had been the Poor Clare Convent when they first arrived in 1804. In the first few days, the nuns received two pupils, but in a short time, they had twelve boarders in the house, and one classroom. In those early days, there were three Skerett girls, two Sherlocks, Ellen

Sweetman, Maria Loghlin, Catherine Cashin, Eliza Waldron, Mary Burke, Mary Fottrell, Bidelia Jones, and Mary Fitzgerald. It was here that the three nuns prepared their prospectus for the new school in Rathfarnham, and the fees were to be thirty-five guineas a year for under 12's, and forty guineas a year for over 12's.

The magnificent red-brick Rathfarnham House, built in 1725 for William Palliser, was reputedly designed by Sir Edward Lovett Pearce. It had been vacant for a few years before the nuns arrived, and required some repairs and alterations, including an extra storey, to make it suitable as a convent, novitiate, and girls boarding school, all renamed Loreto House (later called Loreto Abbey). Henceforth, the nuns were known as Loreto Sisters. In 1823, a Free School was also opened, on the north side of what later became St Josephs Wing (near the present day crèche). Over the next century, many granite extensions were added to Loreto House, including a fabulous chapel around 1840, the adjoining novitiate in 1863, and St Josephs in 1869. The latter is on the north side of the main convent, and contained a refectory (diningroom), concert hall, music room, and dormitories on the upper floors. St Anthonys was built as the main school block in 1896, and is almost hidden behind St Josephs – the accommodation comprised four study halls, eight classrooms, and some dormitories. On the other side of St Josephs, fronting the lawn, is St Francis Xavier, built in 1903, as a gym, art room, music room, and science lab – this was extended westwards in 1931 as St Lisieux, to provide accommodation for prelates visiting the International Eucharistic Congress in Dublin in 1932. In 1922, the nuns built a new study block to the west of the novitiate building. The nuns built their own Gas Works in 1870.

In 1837, the nuns bought the neighbouring Red House beside the south-west corner of the front lawn, as accommodation for the convent chaplain. The Valuation Office House Books in the 1840's recorded it as being used as an Infirmary and by Clergyman, size 44 feet wide, 20 feet deep, and 35 feet high (probably three-storey). This building was demolished in the 1970's to make way for the very-modern St Lourdes Nursing Home for the nuns.

In 1981/82, because of structural problems, the interior of the convent building was practically demolished and rebuilt, incorporating a structural steel frame, and replica plasterwork installed. One wonders if the additional storey added by Mother Teresa Ball in 1822, overloaded the original structure.

The most interesting of all the buildings is undoubtedly the chapel, which was designed by Patrick Byrne, with assistance from the famous Augustus Welby Pugin. The church proper comprises the ground and first floors, with nuns refectory underneath, and nuns "cells" on the top floor. There is a wonderful octagonal lantern light over the crossing (junction of nave and sanctuary), which extends up through the nuns quarters, thus allowing them to watch and hear Mass. The private marble altar (Sacred Heart Altar by Hogan) behind the reardos has an alabaster top half, and is so fine in quality, that daylight passes straight through, creating an almost mystical atmosphere. A fine organ occupies one of the transepts, made by the German firm of Georg Stahlhuth from Aachen. There is another organ in the school concert hall, installed in 1934 by W. Meates & Son, who had just taken over the century-old business of Telford & Telford, Charlemont Street, Dublin.

Loreto Abbey closed in 1999, and was sold to a developer. New apartment blocks were built to the rear of the site, but the original stone buildings had not been converted when the "Celtic Tiger" died in 2008. The nuns built a new convent at the rear of the site, opposite their old walled cemetery, which contains a High Cross in memory of Mother Teresa Ball, who died in 1860. The original cemetery was on the north side of the north gate lodge. The old farmyard buildings were demolished to make way for new houses in Stonepark Abbey in the early 1990's.

Archbishop Daniel Murray was instrumental in founding numerous Catholic religious orders, including the Sisters of Charity, the Mercy Sisters, and the Loreto nuns, and when he died in 1852, his heart was preserved in an urn in Loreto Abbey, Rathfarnham, and then transferred in 1999 to the nun's adjoining cemetery. His coffin is in the basement of the Pro-Cathedral in Dublin, while his mitre and silk slippers are in the Heritage Centre in Our Ladys Hospice, Harold's Cross.

No description of Loreto Abbey Rathfarnham would be complete without mentioning the famous Saint Teresa of Calcutta (1910-1997). She was born Gonxha Agnes to Albanian parents in Skopje in Yugoslavia (now in Macedonia). She wanted to work with the Loreto Sisters in India, and came to Loreto Abbey, Rathfarnham, to learn English, from 12th October to 1st December, 1928. She then proceeded to the Loreto Novitiate in Darjelling, India, and took solemn vows in 1937, while she was teaching in Calcutta (Kalkata). The Loreto Sisters were engaged in teaching the daughters of British Army officers, and when in 1947 the British left India and partitioned the country between Hindus and Muslims, she was no doubt appalled at the accompanying bloodshed. She renounced and left the Loreto Sisters in 1948 to help the poor of Calcutta (which was beside Bengal, and subject of much unrest), and founded the Missionaries of Charity in 1950. She paid a visit to Dublin in 1993, a few years before she died in India. She was canonised a Saint in 2016.

Gaelcholaiste an Phiarsaigh, Loreto Abbey, Grange Road
The Department of Education acquired the old Loreto Abbey after the Celtic Tiger died, and a public Gael-Scoil was opened in part of the original Rathfarnham House in 2015, leaving the remainder of the old buildings empty. In 2017, the Gaelscoil built additional prefab classrooms on the front lawn. This is a co-educational non-denominational secondary school, where all subjects are taught through the medium of Irish, and named in memory of Patrick Pearse, who ran St Enda's school, mostly as an Irish-language school, in the present Pearse Museum, also on Grange Road.

Beaufort, Willbrook Road

The Hodgens family occupied Beaufort House for most of the 19th century, and the estate stretched from Grange Road to Willbrook Road, including the site of the Church of the Annunciation. The estate was shown on an 1801 map as Mr Frizell's demesne. In 1911, Hodgens sold the house and some grounds to the McCabes, who owned the Dublin Pure Ice and Cold Storage Company. It seems that McCabe got into some difficulty over a contract with the War Department, although bonded with the Yorkshire Insurance Company, and in 1920, McCabe sold the premises to Thomas Stevens. The Loreto nuns (Hanna Deasy & Others) bought the property in 1925 from the Stevens family, with a two-fold project in mind, firstly the Loreto College of Domestic Science, and secondly, a High School.

Loreto College of Domestic Science Beaufort

By 1926, the Loreto College of Domestic Science opened, advertising the fact that the Whitechurch bus, via Rathmines and Rathgar, passed the College gates. The fee-paying boarding college was aimed at girls above the age of seventeen, who had completed their Secondary education, and were awarded a Certificate for Efficiency in Household Management, by the Department of Education, at the end of the 1-year course. The curriculum comprised Irish, English, Home Topics (Domestic Science), Cookery, Needlework, Laundry Work, Household Management, Physiology, Hygiene, First Aid and Sick Nursing. The girls were able to play hockey and tennis in their spare time. The first principal was a French lady, Mademoiselle Abrate, and she was succeeded by Mother Joan Mooney, a Loreto nun. The college prepared students for the entrance examinations to the three Domestic Science Colleges, namely, St Catherines, Sion Hill, Blackrock, County Dublin, Cathal Brugha Street College, Dublin, and St Angela's College, Sligo. In 1957, Mother Charles McErlean succeed Mother Joan, and she also trained pupils as

Demonstrators, many of whom were employed as Demonstrators by the Electricity Supply Board, to show customers how to operate electric cookers and other modern appliances in the home. By the 1970's the Demonstrators Course was for a two-year period.

The College closed in 1981, and now the beautiful old Beaufort House (with some substantial modern extensions) is the Provincialate office for the Loreto nuns, featuring some beautiful ornate plasterwork on the ceilings, fine marble fireplaces, etc. The old granite gate pillars on Willbrook Road are still standing, leading to the Beaufort housing estate (built 1995) and Beaufort House, although the one nearest the road, with the word College at the top, was probably erected by the nuns in the 1920's.

Loreto High School Beaufort

The stables of the old Beaufort House were converted into a Kindergarten, Junior, and Secondary School, called Loreto High School Beaufort, which opened in 1925. In 1952, some of the stables were demolished, and a new Secondary School was built alongside the Grange Road, with its distinctive mansard-style roof. 1975 saw the building of a 16-classroom main school in the middle of the site, including an assembly hall and library. In the 1990's, the Kindergarten and Junior School were phased out.

Now the secondary school, which is still owned by the Loreto nuns, caters for 640 girls, taught by 44 teachers. Facilities are constantly being improved, and now include a cafeteria and oratory, in addition to all-weather astro-turf hockey pitches.

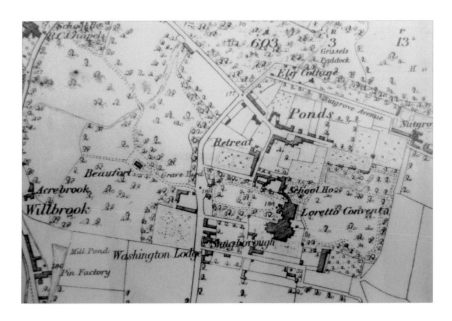

1843 Ordnance Survey map of Lower Rathfarnham. Note the Poor School to the north of Loreto Abbey. (Courtesy of South Dublin Libraries).

Rear of Loreto Abbey, with chapel on left, St Anthony's school block on right.

Amazing translucent alabaster altarpiece in the apse behind the main altar in Loreto Abbey.

Overhead view of two altars in Loreto Abbey chapel.

Interior of Loreto Abbey chapel, with organ in north transept.

Loreto students pray in Loreto Abbey chapel, looking towards south transept. (Courtesy of Loreto Archives).

Looking up at the lantern over the crossing in Loreto Abbey chapel, where some of the nun's "cells" were located.

Senior Orchestra, 1955/56, Loreto Abbey. (Courtesy of Loreto Archives).

THE CONCERT HALL.

St Joseph's wing of Loreto Abbey, contained the Concert Hall.
(Courtesy of Loreto Archives).

THE RECEPTION ROOM.

Reception room in Loreto Abbey convent. (Courtesy of Loreto Archives).

THE ENTRANCE HALL.

Convent entrance hall in Loreto Abbey. (Courtesy of Loreto Archives).

Beaufort House as seen from Loreto Abbey

Wonderful display of articles produced (rugs, embroidery, clothes, etc) in the Beaufort College of Domestic Science. (Courtesy of Loreto Archives).

Schools

Government Report

The 1835 Report of the Commissioners of Public Instruction in Ireland recorded four main schools in Rathfarnham:

1. Daily school of the London Hibernian Society (Anglican), run by Robert Beatty and his wife, charging one penny a week (1d) to the 38 males and 40 females.

2. Daily school, run by Michael Scott, charging between 3d and 8d a week, with the support of the Rector (Anglican).

3. Loreto nuns school, charging 1d a week to 145 girls (this was the Poor School started in 1823).

4. Chapel School (Catholic), run by John Martin, supported by the proceeds of an annual Charity Sermon (people paid to listen to a noted preacher). This was on Willbrook Road.

Anglican National Schools, Main Street

There were two Anglican schools in the early decades of the 19th century, one on Main Street supported by the Rector, and the other at the west end of Church Lane, promoted by the London Hibernian Society, the latter aimed at educating Catholics as well as Protestants. There is an interesting map, dated 1801, plotted by John Byrne, entitled "A Survey of the Lands of Rathfarnham........belonging to the General Fund of the Protestant Dissenters". On this 1801 map, Church Lane is shown as Back Lane, with the Free School at the west end, listed at plot 75 as "Free School & Garden, part of Mr George Bruce's holding." Plot 76 is across the lane, diagonally opposite the school, and listed as

"Factory belonging to the Free School". Archer recorded in 1801 that the school was under Robert Toole. In 1824, there were 30 children, Protestant and Catholic. The Free School is listed in the street directory of 1835 as being run by Robert Beatty. An old house called Tourville is nowadays on the same site, and may have been the original school.

A Government Report of 1821 records that there was only one parish school, with 9 males and 9 females, supported by the Rector, and a small weekly charge from the pupils. They did not mention the London Hibernian Society School. By the time of the 1837 Ordnance Survey map, the parish school is marked as a very small building to the south-east of the church, opening on to Main Street.

The Valuation Office House Book, prepared in the 1840's, records a new building, with house at front, and boys and girls school behind, and there is no mention of the London Hibernian Society School on Church Lane.

The Board of Education files for 1859, record a boys classroom, 20 feet by 17 feet, and a girls classroom of 21 feet by 16 feet, with three windows in each classroom, 4 feet by 2½ feet each. On the date of an inspection, there was no master, and Olivia Gracey, aged 38, presided over 5 boys and 11 girls.

Files for 1895 record one large classroom, 45 feet by 19 feet by 13 feet high, which roughly equates to the two former classrooms being knocked together, with 14 boys and 17 girls.

The school building closed in 1962, and the few remaining children were taught in the War Memorial Hall in Terenure (opposite the west end of Bushy Park Road), where they stayed until their new school opened in 1971 on Washington Lane, off Butterfield Avenue. The latter was extended in 1990, and now caters for 230 children (boys and girls).

In 1994, the old single-storey school was converted into the Parish Centre, linked to the east transept of the church, and the former teacher's house (by that stage used by the sexton) was refurbished for the curate (but nowadays is let as a two-bed house). When the school was surveyed prior to this work, the house had two rooms on both floors, with a central staircase, plus a galley kitchen and a bathroom to the south of the main classroom (probably a former yard). The second classroom was set back from the main façade of the school.

Seemingly, the main classroom was entered via the house hall door on Main Street, and the second classroom was accessed from the doorway at the west end of the school façade, in effect separate entrances for boys and girls. Each classroom had a fireplace. As part of the 1994 project, a ground floor house window facing the church carpark was converted into a doorway.

St Marys Girls National School, Convent Lane, Grange Road

Loreto Free School was established in 1823, to the north of Loreto House (Abbey). When the Loreto nuns applied to the Board of Education in 1834 to be taken-in-charge, the Free School was described as being stone built, with a slated roof, and consisted of one classroom, 37 feet by 10 feet, with six large windows. The classroom could accommodate about 100 children, and some of them paid 1d (one penny) a week. Lewis in 1837 said that the girls received a free suit of clothes annually. In the 1840's, the Valuation Office recorded a building 22 feet wide, 22 feet deep, and 17 feet high (probably two-storey), with an extension of 17 feet wide, 22 feet deep, and 9 feet high.

By at least 1860, a new school had been built, and an 1864 Ordnance Survey map shows it to south of Red House (lately a modern building used as a nursing home for the nuns). The nuns started an Industrial Department in the school in 1860, teaching girls and adults sewing and embroidery, dress-making, etc, with items being sold to provide an income for the students. This was at a time of high unemployment in the locality, because many of the paper and cloth mills were closing down. The Industrial Department had two classrooms, each about 57 feet by 16 feet, seemingly one on the ground floor and another on the first floor.

In 1875 the National School moved to a new building, about 100 yards to the south-east of the nuns chapel, where it remains to this day. The granite-faced, two-storey building is flat-roofed now, although originally had a slated pitched roof, with chimney stacks. Various new buildings have been erected over the years, to accommodate the present 540 girls.

Nutgrove Girls National School, Loreto Avenue
Our Lady of Loreto Girls National School was opened in 1954 by the Loreto Sisters, to cater for the new Local Authority housing estates being built at that time, and included a Secondary Top from 1962 (this meant that pupils could study for the Intermediate Certificate, before the introduction of free Secondary Education in 1967). The single-storey section beside the entrance gates was built at the same time as the school, as a Community Centre for the new residents, and is still going strong. The school closed in 1989, and joined the Good Shepherd National School in Whitehall Road later that year.

Rathfarnham Educate Together, a co-educational, non-denominational National School, took over the Loreto buildings in 1993, having been founded in 1990 at St Marys Anglican church in Crumlin, calling themselves South City School Project.

Ballyroan Boys National School, Ballyroan Road
This seemingly modern school can trace its origins back to Willbrook Road in Rathfarnham village, since in 1821, and probably earlier, there was a school room on Willbrook Road, attached to the Catholic chapel (in those days, the word "church" was only applied to Anglican buildings). The Catholic Directory for 1821 records a Parochial School in the Rathfarnham Chapel enclosure, where 100 boys are educated and clothed (note the last word). The annual Charity Sermon to raise funds for this school was held on the 2nd Sunday in July.

The official Visitation Reports for 1830 and 1833 record John Martin as the master, in charge of about 100 boys (only 60 in Winter!).

The Government introduced National Education in 1831, but it wasn't until 1842, that Fr Laurence Roche, Parish Priest, applied to the new Board of Education for funding for the existing school. The one-roomed building was listed at 41 feet by 11 feet, with a height of 6½ feet to 10 feet (highest under the ridge), and had five windows.

The Valuation Office House Book, prepared in the 1840's, records a school house beside the chapel, being 43 feet long, 14 feet breadth, and 6 feet high, with an addition of 23 feet by 16 feet by 8 feet, and a privy (toilet) of 4 feet by 4 feet by 5 feet.

The school was rebuilt on the same site in 1869, with a grand church-like appearance, of top quality design and workmanship, using the best of granite, and incorporating King Post roof trusses to create an airy interior.

In 1915, a rear flat-roofed extension of 700 square feet was built, abutting and parallel to the rear wall, comprising two extra classrooms. An earlier proposal to convert the basic coach-house into classrooms had been rejected by the Board of Education.

The school stayed on Willbrook Road until 1968, when the school was closed, and the boys moved up to the brand-new Ballyroan National School, which was intended for the newly developing Ballyroan housing estates. Nowadays, there are about 300 boys in the school.

St Marys Boys National School, Grange Road
In 1971, St Mary's Girls National School on Convent Lane began to operate St Mary's Boys National School alongside the girls school, and the boys section expanded into two prefabs in 1973, with two extra classrooms in the old Willbrook Boys School from 1975. In January 1977, a new school was opened behind the Church of the

Annunciation, and St Mary's Boys National School moved into their new premises. Nowadays, the school has 468 boys on the rolls. The land for this new school was originally part of the Beaufort estate, and was bought by the Loreto nuns in 1925 for their new schools. Likewise, the Catholic church was built on Beaufort land.

The school is home to the Rathfarnham Concert Band, founded in 1980, which has junior, intermediate and adult divisions, and they frequently perform concerts in the National Concert Hall, etc.

Santa Maria College Complex, Ballyroan Crescent

"Ballyroan", an old house built in the 1850's, and 53 acres of farmland (including cows and chickens), was gifted by the McCabe family to the Sisters of Mercy, to be used for charitable work, and they initially used it as a working girls hostel cum holiday home, St Marys Convent, which opened in July 1932. On the west side of the convent was a U-shaped stable yard, and parts were rebuilt as a two-storey hostel for the girls, plus a single-storey section as a diningroom and sittingroom. Due to the Second World War ("The Emergency") food shortages, the hostel closed in 1941 and remained empty for about two years.

The Irish Red Cross was very active in the 1940's in trying to eradicate Tuberculosis (TB), and appointed the Sisters of Mercy to run a TB Preventorium for children under the age of five (which age was later increased to twelve), which was to be funded by the Irish Red Cross and various Local Authorities. The idea was to prevent poor children from developing the disease beyond the initial primary stages, by giving them good food, plenty of fresh air, and some drugs where necessary. The Red Cross paid for the former girls hostel to be converted into a small hospital. The hospital opened in September 1943, with twenty beds, staffed by 12 nuns, 12 nurses, and 9 maids, all living on the premises. The children were transferred from St Ultans Hospital in Charlemont

Street, Temple Street Childrens Hospital, and the Richmond Hospital in North Brunswick Street. The following year, the building was extended for a further 15 beds. In September 1947, another big wing was opened to provide 40 additional beds, and nurses quarters, having been built by the Fairyhill Hospital of Howth, bringing the total capacity of the entire hospital to 75 small children. The new wing was a long single-storey building, facing south to the Dublin Mountains, with a terrace for recreation and open-air sleeping. The wards were divided with glass screens to minimise "cross-infution". After fifteen years of fruitful work, the hospital closed in 1958. The Irish Red Cross had a similar hospital at St Raphaels in Cork.

Following the closure of the hospital, the Mercy nuns developed the extensive grounds as a number of schools, to cater for the expanding housing estates being developed in Ballyroan.

In 1960, the nuns converted the Red Cross Preventorium into Santa Maria College, and the initial intake was 38 boys and girls in the National School, and 23 boarders plus 11 day girls in the Secondary School. An Assembly Hall was built in 1963. The National School closed in 1966, when the nuns built Scoil Naomh Padraig girls Primary School on the adjoining site. Around 1969, boarding in the Secondary School was phased out, and gradually, various prefabs were built to cater for increased numbers, until a big extension was built in 1980 at the west end of the school site. Within the last few years, additional buildings have been added around the west blocks. Most of the former TB Preventorium was demolished in early 2019 to make way for a sports hall, hockey courts, and staff car parking, but retaining the original courtyard buildings beside the former convent. Now there are about 520 girls, and 34 teachers.

The convent and some land was sold to Ballyboden St Endas GAA club in 2001, and they built all-weather pitches here, to complement their other facilities in Firhouse Road and elsewhere. The Santa Maria students share the pitches with the GAA club. The club has leased the original convent building to

"Saplings", a school for special-needs children, and the old building still has beautiful plaster cornices in the ground floor rooms, but the original fireplaces are gone. The large walled garden has a nice playground for the school children, and a separate section caters for a "Mens Shed" and allotments for vegetables and flowers. The original TB Preventorium buildings beside the house are used as changing rooms by the GAA players, and the Santa Maria girls.

To the north-east of Santa Maria College is Colaiste Eanna, a Boys Secondary School, initially run by the Christian Brothers, but since 1987, has had a lay principal, and is now under the control of the Edmund Rice Trust (the founder of the Irish Christian brothers). The Brothers bought 13 acres of land from the adjoining Sisters of Mercy, for the sum of £24,710, and the initial school which opened in 1967 was in a prefab, until a permanent building was erected ten years later. Various extensions and new buildings have been added over the decades, and now there are 620 boys, and 47 teachers.

There is another older house off Ballyroan Heights, called "Ballyroan House", not to be confused with the Mercy convent, called "Ballyroan".

Whitechurch National School
The Boys and Girls National School opened in 1823 in the grounds of a future church, which was built four years later. The school had ground floor classrooms, with teacher's residence upstairs. A large classroom, 53 feet by 23 feet by 11 feet high, was added to the rear a decade or two later, with four windows in the east elevation, and one window in each of the gable walls, and probably a central pot-bellied stove for heat. The school closed in 1968, but re-opened in 1978, with additional classrooms in prefabs and the former stables on the south side of the church. The present school was built opposite the Moravian Cemetery in

1990, and has since been extended. The original old school is now the residence of the church sexton, while the rear extension to that school is now the Parochial Centre, after rebuilding and extensions in 1998.

Scoil Mhuire, Whitechurch Green
This National School was built in the early 1980's, and is probably the youngest in the Rathfarnham area.

Edmondstown National School
The original Boys and Girls National School was listed in 1845 by the Valuation Office as being 65 feet by 23 feet by 10 feet high, with a classification of 1B⁺, meaning a slated stone building, not very old, in good repair. The school was abandoned in the 1950's, and was demolished in recent years to allow for the construction of the M50 motorway overhead. The present school opened in 1954, alongside the picturesque Owendoher River, and was recently extended.

Divine Word National School, Marley Grange
The Divine Word National School opened in 1978 on land donated by the Loreto nuns, as a single-storey building, and has been extended with a two-storey block.

St Columba's College, Whitechurch
This famous secondary boarding school for boys was founded in 1843 in Stackallan House, between Navan and Slane, County Meath. The founders comprised four Protestant landowners and four Protestant clergymen, although the lay founders left after a few years. The college has always been managed by the Warden, who was a clergyman, until a layman was appointed in 1974.

Stackallan proved to be unsuitable, and in 1849 the college moved to 18th century Holly Park on 100 acres, south of Rathfarnham, which had been built by Lundy Foot, a tobacco and snuff merchant of Parliament Street in Dublin. This very substantial two-storey over basement house is five bays wide, but very deep at seven bays. The outer hall contains very fine black-stained wood panelling which was brought from Stackallan House. The full depth inner hall has some fine ornate ceiling plasterwork.

The school immediately built the Dining Hall, Dormitories, a temporary timber-framed chapel, and temporary classrooms. The Cloisters were added in 1852, and dormitories built above the Dining Room in 1862. The Big Schoolroom was built in 1875, but was substantially rebuilt after a major fire in 1896. The detached Chapel dates from 1880, and features some nice stained glass windows. The exceptionally large chapel bell, cast in 1844, is housed in a bellcote, and was donated to the Stackallan school by Warden Singleton (Rev. R.C. Singleton). Local granite is the main material for most of these additions, with some elements of sandstone, especially in the chapel. The small Masterman Library (now the Career Guidance Room) was the last of the old-style buildings to be erected in 1919, and the internal plasterwork contains the cut hair from all the pupils at that time – normally horsehair would have been used to strengthen the lime plaster, but the horse population had been wiped out in the battlefields of the First World War.

Up until 1969, the college was self-sufficient, with its own farm, and even a gasworks before the advent of electricity.

In recent decades, various new classroom and accommodation blocks have been built for students and staff, in campus style, including a sports hall, although the Victorian chapel is still a focal point in school life.

The site now extends to 140 acres, and includes the Kilmashogue Golf Club, for use of former and current students. There is plenty of space for cricket, rugby, tennis, and even an outdoor swimming pool. Currently there are about 250 students, male and female (girls were first admitted to senior classes in 1971), Protestants and Catholics, mostly boarders, and soutanes and surplices are worn by the students on various occasions.

Rockbrook Park School, Edmondstown Road

This fee-paying boys Secondary school was founded by a group of teachers and parents in 1971, in a rented premises at 114-116 St Stephens Green, and they purchased Rockbrook House in 1975. The house dates from the middle of the 18th century, with modest proportions and features suitable for the owner of the paper mill near the house. The Campbell family acquired the property in 1941, and replaced the rear annex with a new wing. Bungalow-style classrooms were built near the old house in 1980, and then a spacious modern block to the south of the site was erected in 2008, leaving the old house for administration, and an oratory. The school has two grass football pitches, three astro-turf hockey pitches, and two tennis courts. The Owendoher River (Glendoo Branch) flows through the grounds, although at a much lower level, affording plenty of walks and adventure for the students. There are currently 180 boys on the rolls.

Rockbrook was a village in the days when millworkers were numerous, with its own single-storey National School. The latter is now a private house, and immediately behind it is the old section of Cruagh Cemetery, actually a mound, with a low Round Tower on top. Old maps show a ruined church alongside the tower. The tower is reputed to be a Watch Tower, to ward off "body-snatchers", although it is probably only a folly.

Former Nutgrove Boarding School, Nutgrove Avenue

This school is reputed to have been built in 1802, and continued as a boarding school until about 1876. During the 20th century, it was listed as a private house, known to locals as the "White House". The Church of the Annunciation used the building for a while as a Parish Office, before it was demolished around 1970.

The site has been empty since then, except for the Scout Hall. Up until the 1950's, Nutgrove Avenue was a cul-de-sac ending at this school, but was widened and extended to link up with Churchtown.

Carnegie Library, Taylors Lane

Andrew Carnegie was a Scottish philanthropist, who made a fortune in the steelworks of America, and set up the Carnegie Trust to distribute some of his wealth for building libraries and other educational endeavours. A substantial amount of money was allocated to Ireland, and many libraries were built in the first years of the 20th century. Rathfarnham was granted funding, but unfortunately an unsuitable site was chosen, out in the middle of nowhere, when it opened in 1911. The fine design and workmanship of the single-storey granite and red brick building, with red tiled roof, is much admired. At one stage, a caretaker occupied a tiny apartment behind the diocletian windows above the entrance doorway. Now the building is partly used by local community groups, following closure two years ago.

A state-of-the-art €4million new library was opened in Ballyroan in 2013, replacing the first 1985 library.

Ballyroan Library, 2010. (Courtesy of South Dublin Libraries).

Loreto Girls National School was built in its third location in 1875, and originally had a pitched and slated roof.

Loreto Girls National School, 1948/49. (Courtesy of Seamus Kelly).

Loreto National School Sports Day, about 1970. Stonepark Abbey houses were later built in this field. (Courtesy of Seamus Kelly).

Old Edmondstown National School before 1954, with diamond-shaped window panes. (Courtesy of Seamus Kelly).

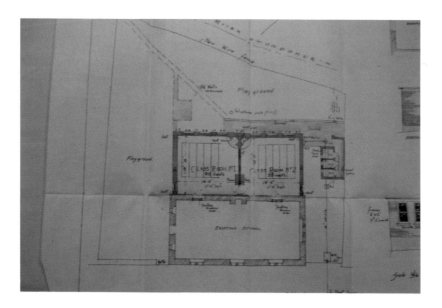

Rathfarnham Boys National School on Willbrook Road was rebuilt in 1869, and extended to the rear in 1915. Later used as a Courthouse, and now the Parochial Hall. (Courtesy of National Archives of Ireland).

Rathfarnham Boys National School, Willbrook Road, 1925. Note the horse in the field in the background. (Courtesy of Seamus Kelly).

Single-storey Anglican National School and two-storey teachers residence on Main Street was built in the 1840's, and now partly used as the Parish Centre.

The focal point of St Columba's College is the 18th century Holly Park mansion, which is traditionally used by the Warden (college manager).

St Columba's College. Side of Holly Park on right, Dining Hall/Stackallan House in centre, and Big School Room on left.

St Columba's College. Famous cloisters under the Dining Room.

1919 Masterman Library in St Columba's College. The internal wall plaster is reinforced with boy's hair, following a visit by the school barber.

Outer hall of Holly Park, St Columba's College contains carved wood panelling from Stackallan House in County Meath.

Aerial view of Santa Maria College, with former convent on right, and the former Red Cross TB Preventorium in centre. (Courtesy of Mercy Archives).

Santa Maria College was the Red Cross TB Preventorium in the 1940's and 1950's. This part was demolished in early 2019. (Courtesy of Mercy Archives).

Santa Maria College. The former stables beside the Mercy nuns convent were initially a Girls Hostel in the 1930's, and then the Red Cross TB Preventorium. Now used by St Endas Ballyboden GAA club as changing rooms. In the photo below, the sick children were required to get plenty of fresh air. (Courtesy of Mercy Archives).

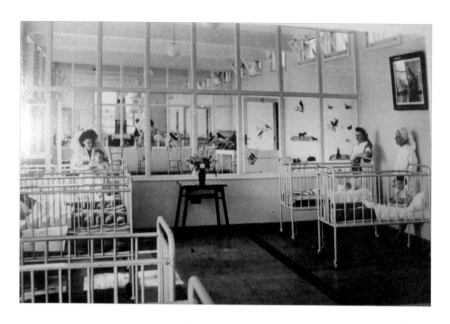

Santa Maria College. The 1947 wing of the Red Cross TB Preventorium. (Courtesy of Mercy Archives).

Santa Maria College, with the Mercy nuns convent. Note the oratory window on the left. (Courtesy of Mercy Archives).

Rockbrook Park School. The Georgian house is now the administration block, with the modern school to the rear.

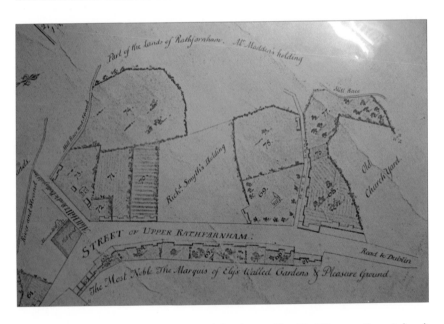

Byrne's 1801 map of Main Street, Rathfarnham. Plot No 75 was a Free School supported by the London Hibernian Society. (Courtesy of Trinity College Dublin Map Library)

Churches

Rathfarnham Parish Church (Anglican), Main Street

The ruins of the original church are still in the old graveyard to the south of the Texaco petrol station. The church was Catholic until the Reformation in the 16th century, when it was allocated to the new Church of Ireland (also called the Established Church). The earliest legible headstone records a death in 1689.

The present charming church, with its unorthodox layout, originally opened in 1789 (dedicated in 1795) as one rectangular building on a north-south axis, with the altar in the centre of the long west wall. In those days, the raised pulpit was directly behind the altar. The north tower, spire, and vestry were added in 1821, following receipt of a loan of £900 from the Board of First Fruits. The east transept, and north stepped gallery, date from 1852 (the original organ, donated by Edward Blackburne of Rathfarnham Castle, was installed in 1854 in this transept), and the much shallower west transept was added in 1889 to house the new organ, necessitating moving the altar to the south end of the nave. This new organ, made by Forster & Andrews of Hull, was the gift of the Tottenham family in Ashfield House.

A small side chapel was built in 2001, on the west side of the tower/porch. At the same time, a former basement crypt in this area was converted into a homely Columbarium, with a variety of cremation urns (each named) on the former coffin shelves. There are now plans to build a columbarium garden on the north side of the church carpark.

Most windows are fitted with lovely stained glass, some old, some modern, the earliest dating from 1890, when the altar was re-sited. There are two from Munich, two from Watson & Co of Youghal, one from Earley & Company of Camden Street, two modern ones from Irish Stained Glass Company, and "The Good

Shepherd" from Hubert McGoldrick of An Tur Gloine in Dublin in 1928.

Contrary to popular belief, there are no bells in the belltower (although there is plenty of space), and parishioners are called to service by means of a recording and loudspeakers fitted behind the tower louvres! However, annual accounts in the past recorded payments to the bell-ringer, so presumably the original church bell was removed at some stage.

In 1993, the old schoolhouse was extended westwards to link up with the church, for use as a Parish Centre, and the former teachers house fronting Main Street was refurbished for use by the curate (although today is let on the open market as a two-bedroom house).

Originally Rathfarnham was part of Taney parish in Dundrum, but became a separate parish in 1851.

The Rectory is located in Terenure, a large detached house directly behind the War Memorial Hall/Parochial Hall (opposite the west end of Bushy Park Road). The Hall was opened in 1923, in memory of those Protestant parishioners who died in the First World War. Much to their credit, the Shaw family of Bushy Park donated a large timber Celtic cross in 1924, in memory of all Catholics and Protestants who died in that war.

Until the Irish Church Act of 1869 was implemented in 1871, all Irish people paid for the upkeep of the Established Church (Anglican), whether they were Protestant or Catholic, by means of Tithes (taxes). After the introduction of the Act, the Anglicans were no longer state-supported.

Whitechurch (Anglican), Whitechurch Road
The original ruined church and graveyards can still be seen at the south end of Grange Brook Vale.

The present simple and graceful granite church, with charming slender spire, and narrow lancet windows, was consecrated on the 3rd June, 1827 by the Rev. Lundy Foot. John

Semple was the architect, but Thomas Drew was responsible for the 1868 chancel and organ chamber, while the vestry was added in 1876. The rear gallery was inserted in 1834, and extended in 1993 to accommodate an additional organ. Timber-framed diaphragm arches, plastered to look like masonry, support the roof.

The original windows, with diamond-shaped panes, were replaced with new plain windows in 1988. The north-east stained-glass window is the work of Joshua Clarke & Sons, North Frederick Street, the father of Harry Clarke.

There are two organs, one disused in the chancel (Brown & Company, St Stephens Green, Dublin, with hand-operated bellows), and the other (1890's by Peter Conacher & Company, Huddersfield & Dublin) on the rear gallery, which came from St Mary's Anglican Church, Ballinrobe, County Mayo, in 1993 (the former church is now used as the public library). Some pipes from the former Mariner's Church in Dun Laoghaire were incorporated into the 1993 rebuilding of the gallery organ.

Whitechurch Vicarage on Grange Road, a house formerly called Ormond, was purchased in 1902, but Grange Wood estate is now on the site. The present 1966 vicarage is immediately to the north of the Moravian Cemetery on Whitechurch Road.

The well-kept cemetery surrounding the church contains the graves of many notable Rathfarnham residents, such as La Touche, Tedcastle, and Love, all from Marlay demesne. In fact, the La Touche underground vaults date from 1805, before the church was built. Tedcastle has an underground vault behind the church chancel, and also a conventional grave to the north. Other names include, Catherine Amelia O'Brien (stained glass artist from An Tur Gloine studio), Annie Smithson (author of "The Weldons of Tibradden", and other works), Jolly (local dairy), Hughes (HB Ice Cream), Dr Albert Croly (dispensary doctor), Custis (publican), Rowley (Marley Grange), Guinness, Taylors (Harold's Grange), and many more. The graveyard was extended in 1970.

There are two cemeteries associated with the old Whitechurch church, at Grange Brook Vale, which are labelled on old maps as the La Touche Burying Ground. Access is via a narrow lane off the Whitechurch Road. The main cemetery surrounds the ruined church. The other small walled cemetery is across the lane, backing on to the house called Palmyra, and near the gate are the headstones of the Harty family – Sir Robert Way Harty, Bart., was Lord Mayor of Dublin in 1831.

Church of the Annunciation, Willbrook Road

The original medieval Catholic church was behind the present Texaco petrol station at the north-west end of Main Street, and was reputed to have been dedicated to St Peter & St Paul, but it fell under Protestant control after the Reformation in the 1530's.

Rev. Myles V. Ronan wrote that there was a Mass House in Rathfarnham in 1697, under the care of Rev. Timothy Kelly, who lived in Oldcastle. He goes on to say that Rev. Nicholas Gibbons was living in Rathfarnham in 1730, and that a cottage had been converted into a Chapel in that same year. Chapel was the term applied to Catholic places of worship after the Reformation, and Church denoted an Anglican place of worship. Methodists and Presbyterians were also designated as chapels. It is probable that the cottage conversion lasted no more than a few decades, and no doubt, a proper chapel was built in due course.

Francis Ball, writing in 1905 about the history of County Dublin, reports that during the tenure of Fr Robert Bethel (1766-1781), an amount of £200 was stolen from the main church in Tallaght, which was intended for an extension to the church in Rathfarnham. An 1801 map shows the chapel on Willbrook Road (plot 26a on that map). The Duncan map of 1821, also shows the chapel on the west side of Willbrook Road. The Catholic Directory for 1821 records Rev. Nicholas Kearns as Parish Priest, assisted by Fr Laurence Roach, and one officiating curate. Samuel Lewis, writing in 1837, said that there was a large chapel, with a good house for the priest nearby. Dalton describes the chapel in 1838 as "cruciform edifice with galleries disproportionately low".

The 1830 official Visitation Report, records a silver chalice and silver ciborium, and four suits of vestments (one black, and three coloured). There was a "very indifferent" Parochial House, with a coach house, cow house, and stable, but no glebe (land). Brethren could borrow books from the parish library.

The 1833 official Visitation Report, records that the chapel was dedicated to St Peter, and that the rent was £4 a year. This time, there are six suits of vestments, three albs, and one cape, in addition to three sets of altar linen. There were 100 books in the parish library. Two religious societies, one purgatorian and one for Catholic Doctrine, taught doctrine every Sunday after Mass.

The 1840's Valuation Office House Books provide a valuable record of St Peters Chapel, giving the following dimensions (length, breadth, height): Main section is 22 feet by 68 feet by 20 feet, Centre is 44 feet by 24 feet by 20 feet, More is 27 feet by 25 feet by 20 feet, Staircase is 9 feet by 22 feet by 17 feet. The return section was 45 feet by 18 feet by 15 feet, plus a staircase of 5 feet by 6 feet by 7 feet. The classification was generally 1B, meaning a slated stone or brick building, not new, but in good repair. Fr Laurence Roach's substantial two-storey house is either adjacent or abutting the chapel, being 27 feet by 32 feet by 18 feet, with a 9 feet by 5 feet by 18 feet porch, a return of 24 feet by 7 feet by 15 feet, another return of 18 feet by 17 feet by 16 feet. His car stable was 20 feet by 17 feet by 12 feet, the stable was 28 feet by 17 feet by 12 feet, and there were a few stores and sheds.

Fr Theobald Mathew, the famous Cork temperance priest, preached in St Peters Chapel and gave the "pledge" after the 12.30pm Mass on the 8th March, 1846.

In the 1870's, a plot of land for the present Church of the Annunciation was donated by the Hodgens family of Beaufort House. The foundation stone was laid in 1875, and the attractive granite-faced church was dedicated in 1878. The architect was George Ashlin, and the builder was Michael Meade & Sons.

The main marble altar was made by Farrell & Sons, while the side altars, communion rail and statues were the work of Patrick O'Neill & Company, Great Brunswick Street (now called Pearse Street). Some of the stained glass windows date from the 1870's, but the Stations of the Cross windows are later, and are the work of Maison Denis or Eugene Denis of Nantes, France. Unfortunately, the gold mosaics around altars were painted over at some stage. The stone holy water font outside the entrance came from the old St Peters Chapel on Willbrook Road.

The site of the old St Peters Chapel, bordering on the much lower Owendoher River, was used to build a new Presbytery in the 1880's, called St Marys, and also for the present parochial car park, all surrounded by majestic giant redwood trees. The present Parochial Hall was formerly the National School on the chapel site. Interestingly, the presbytery is actually a pair of semi-detached houses, with different bay windows, and hall doors in different locations (one on the front, and one on the side).

Church of the Divine Word, Marley Grange Estate

The Catholic parish of Rathfarnham originally included the Churchtown region until 1965, and a Chapel-of-Ease was built in 1957, called the Church of the Good Shepherd. Churchtown then became responsible for Marlay Grange from 1974 to 1981, when the Church of the Divine Word was built in 1981 on land donated by the Loreto nuns. Interestingly, the free-standing outside bell is dated 1933, and presumably came from another church.

The Servite priests came to Benburb, County Tyrone, in 1947, and bought Elm Park House beside Marlay Park in 1975, for use as a novitiate. They took over Marlay parish in 1992. The Servites have also been running the lovely oratory on the 1st floor of Rathfarnham Shopping Centre since the 1990's, still aided by a band of merry volunteers.

Elm Park House was sold by the Landed Estates Court in 1862, and the particulars stated that the house was a modern one, with three reception rooms and seven bedrooms. A waterwheel on the river pumped water to a cistern on the roof, which in turn supplied the water-closet (toilet), and also the fountain in the garden, and the greenhouses and hothouse. There was also an external water pipe, to which a hose could be attached in the event of the house catching fire. Another owner around 1898 established a racecourse on the 30 acres, including a grandstand. Grange Wood housing estate was built on part of the Servite land in recent decades, and finally, the house, on 2½ acres, was sold by the Servites in 1997, with Planning Permission for 16 apartments.

Our Lady of Good Counsel, Whitechurch Green

The Augustinian priests came to Ireland in the late 13th century, but dispersed to Europe after the Reformation in the 16th century, and returned in the 19th century. "John's Lane" in Thomas Street is probably their most famous church, although its proper name is Church of St Augustine & St John.

In 1872 the priests purchased "Orlagh" on Old Court Road below the Hellfire Club, for use as their novitiate. This was a fine period property, built around 1790 by the Foot family (who became famous in the 19th century for their snuff and tobacco factory in Parliament Street), and extended a few times over the years. This house eventually proved unsuitable, and in 1948 they bought another house in Raheny in north Dublin for students.

With the prospect of UCD moving to Belfield, the priests bought St Catherines, at the corner of Taylors Lane and Edmondstown Road in 1955, and built a new student residence, for those junior priests who would attend lectures in UCD.
In 1973, the priests were asked to take over the new parish of Ballyboden, and initially were able to share their student oratory with their parishioners. The new church, Our Lady of Good Counsel, was completed in 1981. The old holy water font on the right of the altar came from their abbey in Tullow, County Carlow.

Pride of place must go to the small bell in the tower, which came from the Church of Santa Maria, Posterula, Rome, and which was cast in 1612, and is inscribed to Pope Paul the Fifth.

The St Catherines student accommodation was by now empty, because of the fall-off in vocations to the priesthood, and in 1983, the priests leased it to the Eastern Health Board (now the HSE), and that same year, built themselves a new monastery at the back of the site. The HSE vacated the building about five years ago, and currently, the priests are selling the large site and former novitiate, including the Pitch & Putt course surrounding it.

Orlagh on the Old Court Road was used as a Retreat House until recent years, when it was bought by local investors.

Church of Holy Spirit, Marian Road, Ballyroan

This large modern church was built in 1967, and features two large Sean Keating murals, stained glass "Stations of the Cross" by Murphy Davitt Studios, Dublin, marble-work by Earley of Camden Street, and a pipe organ by R.E. Meates, Dublin. Una Craddock created the metal sculpture on the front elevation. A hollow in the foundation stone contains a fragment of granite from the old church in Rathfarnham (presumably the one which was on the present Presbytery site on Willbrook Road).

Quaker Meeting House, Crannagh Road

The site was donated in 1957 by Lamb Bros, who were Quakers (Religious Society of Friends), and had operated a fruit farm on the south side of Rathfarnham village. The Meeting House & Social Centre was built that same year, and comprised a tall badminton hall, with the actual prayer meeting room in the single-storey wing of the building. Nowadays, the badminton hall is sublet to other local groups, such as crèche, etc.

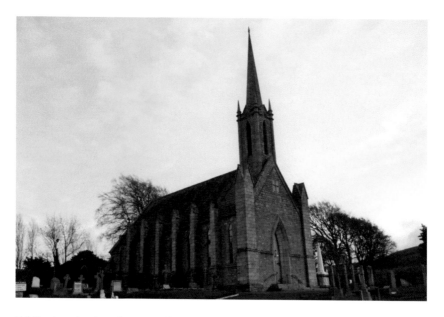

Whitechurch church opened in 1827, four years after the National School fronting the main road.

The pleasant interior of Whitechurch church.

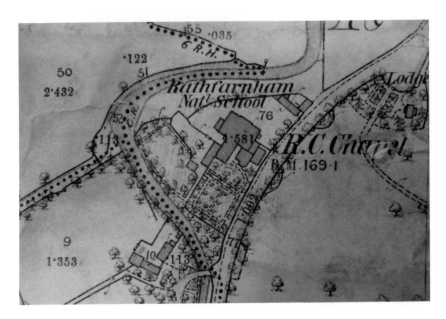

1864 Ordnance Survey map, showing the original Catholic chapel (T-shaped), and probably the abutting presbytery underneath the numeral 8, with garden attached. The former Dispensary was just below the River Owendoher. (Courtesy of South Dublin Libraries).

Impressive interior of Church of the Annunciation.

Cosy interior of Anglican church on Main Street, with organ in west transept.

The empty Augustinian novitiate at the corner of Taylors Lane and Edmondstown Road is now for sale, including the Pitch & Putt course.

The Quakers Sports Hall and Meeting House on Crannagh Road.

The ruins of the Christian church at the north end of Main Street were in better shape a few decades ago, but now have almost disappeared. (Courtesy of South Dublin Libraries).

St Enda's & The Priory

St Enda's Park, Grange Road

Present-day St Enda's Park was shown on a map of 1801 as the Fields of Odin, occupied by Edward Hudson. Hudson, who was the State Dentist, built the house around 1786, as an impressive two-storey over basement mansion, clad with ashlar granite. The Hudsons are credited with building the various small follies around the 50-acre demesne. By the time of the 1837 Ordnance Survey, the house is shown as Hermitage.

Padraig Pearse was born in 1879 in 27 Great Brunswick Street (now called Pearse Street), where his English father carried on a very successful business as ecclesiastical monumental sculptors, and Padraig attended nearby Westland Row Christian Brothers School, before qualifying in 1901 as a barrister. He never practiced law, but after his father died in 1900, Patrick and his artistic brother Willie, carried on the business until it was sold in 1910.

Padraig was more interested in culture and education, and founded Scoil Eanna (St Enda's) in 1908 in his home, Cullenswood House, 21a Oakley Road, Ranelagh. This Catholic boarding school was for boys from the age of five to fifteen, and lessons were mostly taught through Irish. Ranelagh proved to be an unsuitable location, and so, in 1910, the Pearse family (mother, brothers, sisters) leased Hermitage from the landlord, William Woodbyrne. A previous tenant from 1900 was Sir Neville Chamberlaine, Chief Inspector of the Royal Irish Constabulary. With the proceeds of the sale of the business in Great Brunswick Street, Padraig carried out the necessary alterations to make the house suitable as a school, including converting the stables into classrooms. One wing contained the Study Hall, and also a chapel, the latter used only for prayers, since the boys walked to the Church of the Annunciation in Rathfarnham village for Mass, etc. Between 1910 and 1912, Padraig also operated Scoil Ide in Cullenswood House, to cater for girls.

Leading up to 1916, Padraig Pearse was involved in planning the Easter Rising, and the house and grounds were used for various meetings, practice drills, and even bomb-making, although the empty Larkfield Mill in Kimmage (now Tesco supermarket) was also used for the two latter activities. On Easter Monday, 24th April, 1916, Padraig and Willie Pearse, together with some teachers and former pupils, left Scoil Eanna to proclaim the Irish Republic in the General Post Office in the city centre, thus starting the Easter Rising. By mid-May, the two brothers, along with other leaders, had been executed by the British Army in Kilmainham Gaol (Jail), thus hardening sentiment against the British occupation of Ireland. Ironically, Eoin MacNeill, who countermanded the order to start the Rising, lived in nearby Woodtown Park House, near the present Rathfarnham Golf Club.

Mrs Pearse moved Scoil Eanna back to Cullenswood House in Ranelagh after the Rising, because the authorities took over the Hermitage, and she stayed in Ranelagh until 1919, when she was able to return to Rathfarnham, and then bought the property from the landlord in 1920. She continued the school until her death in 1932, and the school closed in 1935. Padraig's sister, Margaret, continued to live in the house until her death in 1968, after which the estate was gifted to the State.

Since 1979, Hermitage has been managed by the Office of Public Works as the Pearse Museum. The charming walled garden to the side of the house contains a central fountain, and the sandstone slabs on the path surrounding it are carved with the words of a poem called "The Wayfarer", composed by Padraig Pearse in 1916. The former school classrooms have been adapted as a café, Nature Room, and mock classroom. The top floor of the house is used for art exhibitions, the ground floor depicts dormitories, dining hall, chapel etc, while the basement tells the life and times of Padraig Pearse. The grounds are now called St Enda's Park, with woods and streams, lawns and football pitches.

An unusual feature of the museum is the rough timber table in the hallway, which is reputed to have been used to cut off Robert Emmet's head, after he was hung in 1803 outside St Catherines Church in Thomas Street, Dublin. As part of the 1916 centenary celebrations, South Dublin County Council unveiled a questionable and unsightly abstract concrete sculpture in 2017, outside the new entrance to St Enda's Park, supposedly replicating the Robert Emmet Table inside the Pearse Museum! Emmet was captured in 1803 in Harold's Cross, and a plaque was affixed to the house site in 2003 to commemorate that event.

Besides the Pearse Museum, the two Pearse brothers are also commemorated by a 1952 bronze plaque in bas-relief on the west balustrade of Pearse Bridge over the River Dodder.

Cullenswood House in Ranelagh has been used since 1996 as Gaelscoil Lios na nOg, a co-educational Primary School.

The Priory, Grange Road

John Philpot Curran was born in Newmarket, County Cork in 1750, and became a famous barrister and personality. He purchased a modest house in Rathfarnham, around 1787, and named it "The Priory". In 1792, one of his daughters, Gertrude, aged 12, fell from an upstairs window and died. Curran was heart-broken, and insisted that her little body be buried in the lawn outside his study window.

Another daughter, Sarah, was in love with Robert Emmet, who was secretly residing in 1803 in Butterfield Avenue (then called Butterfield Lane), but the exact location of the house is not known. Sarah Curran Avenue commemorates her name.

Anne Devlin was a servant to Robert Emmet at this time, and when she was arrested after the 1803 Rebellion, she refused, under torture, to divulge any information about Robert Emmet. However, she was never thanked for her heroism by the public, and died a pauper in 1851. Many decades afterwards, a headstone was erected by Dr. Richard Madden on her grave in

67

Glasnevin, and in 2004 a statue was unveiled in her memory at the south end of Main Street, Rathfarnham, in front of Wolfe Tone Terrace.

John Philpot Curran died in London in 1817, and later his body was re-buried in Glasnevin, Dublin.

The house, "Priory", was occupied by various people, up until about 1930, until it was abandoned and was a ruin by 1959. Nowadays, there are only fragments of a ruin left, in the open space of the 1980 housing estate called Hermitage (not Priory!). The skeleton of Gertrude Curran has never been found, just like that of Robert Emmet.

Pearse Museum, St Enda's Park

1914 prize-giving day at Scoil Eanna (St Enda's), with Padraig Pearse seated near right end. (Courtesy of Pearse Museum/OPW).

Hall of Pearse Museum, with 1803 Robert Emmet be-heading block/table.

Unveiling of sculpture of Anne Devlin on Main Street, Rathfarnham, on the 4th March, 2004.

Marlay Park

In bygone centuries, Harold's Grange, or "The Grange", was originally the seat of the Harold family. In 1764, David La Touche purchased the land and a late 17th century farmhouse, the purchase relying on a lease of 1729 between William Connolly to John Taylor, the latter being a brewer of Marrowbone Lane in The Liberty of Thomas-Court & Donore (off present-day Thomas Street). Thirty years later, La Touche built the present Georgian mansion as an extension on the east side of the farmhouse, while still retaining the latter lower building, re-naming the property shortly afterwards as Marlay House, since Marlay was his wife's maiden name. The stables adjoining the old farmhouse (now the Craft Courtyard) probably date from the La Touche era. The La Touche family, who were Huguenot (French Protestants) immigrants, were initially involved in linen and silk weaving, and later became famous in the banking world, especially the formation of Bank of Ireland. The family burial plots can be seen in the adjoining Whitechurch graveyard, which was once part of Marlay demesne, and also in the old graveyard beside the original Whitechurch church.

In 1864 the 396-acre demesne was sold on the instructions of the Landed Estates Court to the well-known coal-merchant, Robert Tedcastle. The sale particulars stated that the mansion house at that date was temporarily occupied by the Archbishop of Dublin, who was due to vacate on the 1st November, 1864. The particulars also referred to a Bailiffs House on the demesne.

Tedcastle sold a large plot at the north-east corner in 1874 to Rowley, who built Marlay Grange.

In 1924 the estate was bought by Robert Kenton-Love, who was a market-gardener, and was famous for his 5-acres of tomato glasshouses. Some of these were in the three-section walled garden, and others were to the south of the farmyard near the south end of the demesne.

The 300 acre park was bought by Dublin County Council in 1972, and opened to the public in 1975. The splendid house was initially in poor condition, but an eight–year restoration of the main house was completed in 2000. Although the entire house is still unused, part of the ground floor is open for public tours a few times a year, comprising entrance hall (but not the staircase), Breakfast Room, Diningroom/Ballroom, Oval Room, and Library, featuring ornate ceiling plasterwork, fine joinery, quality marble fireplaces, etc.). The former farmhouse is still joined to the main house, and although now restored, is still not open to the public. However, the public can look in some of the windows from the courtyard, and admire the wonderful two-storey kitchen, with its cooking ranges, ovens, etc, and the galleried room on one side. The stable courtyard has been in use for many years as craft studios and shops, but the roofed link cum archway, with bell-cote on top, connecting the original old farmhouse to the stables, was regrettably removed as part of the restoration.

Nowadays, this magnificent public amenity includes five GAA football pitches, six soccer pitches, one all-weather soccer pitch, a cricket ground, a nine-hole par-3 golf course (plus restaurant), tennis courts, a dog park, childrens playgrounds, etc. The park has thousands of mature trees, streams and lakes (the Little Dargle River), expansive lawns, and a multitude of walking paths. The walled garden near the house, includes Tea Rooms, a flower garden, a kitchen garden, an aviary, and a few peacocks wandering at will. The former stables beside the house have been converted into craft studios/retail outlets. Near the remote farmyard, there is a miniature railway, with rides for children on Summer weekends, and also the quaint cottage called Laurelmere in the woods. For the musically minded, Marlay Park is now the venue for the major Longitude Festival every July, when numerous marquees and stages are erected, playing host to the latest pop-idols.

Thanks to the Love family, Evie Hone lived and worked in the Dower House from 1944, after An Tur Gloinne closed. She was a cubist painter, and later concentrated on stained glass. Among her many beautiful stained-glass windows, one of the most popular is probably "My Four Green Fields", depicting the four provinces of Ireland, and now the staircase window in Government Buildings, Upper Merrion Street, Dublin. In March, 1955, aged 61, she collapsed on the street and died immediatly, while on her way to Mass in the Church of the Annunciation in Rathfarnham. Evie contracted polio at a young age, and suffered throughout her life, but she bravely fostered her artistic talents. While living and working in Marlay House, she gave her address as the Dower House. Such a term is applied to a more modest home of a widow, who is forced to leave a mansion house in favour of the male heir, and would often be a nice lodge or good house on the estate. Marlay did not have a Dower House, and she may have applied the title to the original farmhouse attached to the mansion house. She definitely had her studio in the big west room of Marlay House itself (formerly called the Library), but only accessed it via the French window in the big bow window of this room. She lived on the first floor at the north-east corner of the stable yard, and may have used the rough room underneath for her firing-oven, but it was more likely situated in the original farmhouse adjacent (but not connected) to her big studio. In her studios, she employed five staff, two young female general helpers, and three men – glass-cutter, firing-oven operator, and leadwork assembler. In stained-glass windows, the vivid colours are the different colours of the individual pieces of glass, and not the paint, since the images are all painted with a brownish or blackish paint (typically oxide of iron mixed with finely crushed glass and oil or gum), and fused/baked into the coloured glass in a high-temperature oven.

Rear elevation of Marlay House, with original late-17th century farmhouse on left.

Marlay House from the courtyard, with the original late-17th century farmhouse in the centre.

"My Four Green Fields", the wonderful stained-glass window made by Evie Hone in 1939, now graces the staircase of Government Buildings on Upper Merrion Street. It represents the traditional symbols of the four provinces of Ireland: Harp of Leinster, Three Crowns of Munster, Sword/Eagle of Connaught, and Red Hand of Ulster.

Golf Courses

There are four major golf clubs in Rathfarnham, the oldest being Rathfarnham, followed by Grange, Castle and the youngest being Edmondstown, and with the exception of the Castle Golf Club, they practically touch off each other. Initially, members carried their own clubs (sticks) on their backs, until "caddies" (children) were individually employed to do this heavy work, and nowadays, the members can use electric buggies to ferry themselves and their clubs around the course.

Rathfarnham Golf Club, Stocking Lane

In 1899, Patrick Bogue, the tenant in Butterfield House on Butterfield Avenue (currently occupied by The Irish Pharmacy Union), built a 9-hole golf course on 50-acres of land alongside the River Dodder, and invited paying guests to use it. A few local people, including Sir Frederick Shaw of Bushy Park House, formed the Rathfarnham Golf Club, and availed of the new course, using a two-storey cottage as their clubhouse. When Bogues lease expired in 1902, the Club entered into a new lease from 1903, with John McEntaggart, the owner, and immediately built a clubhouse to the west of the bridge over the River Owendoher, near the south end of Main Street. Grazing sheep helped to keep the grass cut in the early days! McEntaggart main occupation was running the Empire Restaurant in Nassau Street.

In 1965, the Club decided that they needed a bigger course, and bought 60 acres of farmland in Newtown, on Stocking Lane, where they laid out another 9-hole golf course, built a new clubhouse, and were ready for play in 1966.

In 1994, extra land was acquired for three more holes, and in 2015, they achieved their dream of a full 18-hole course. The club logo comprises a mill with waterwheel, which is very appropriate, since the Owendoher River fuelled many mills in this locality in the 18th and 19th century.

There is a small National Monument (DU022-115) on the golf course, comprising a Bronze-Age (2,400-500 BC) Fulacht Fia, a cooking pit. Elsewhere on the course, at Hole 9, a partial ruin of Newton Little Mill has been preserved, comprising the gable wall of a single-storey stone building.

After they left Butterfield Avenue in the 1960's, Rathfarnham Shopping Centre was built on part of the old course in 1969, followed by housing estates, Fairways (very appropriate) and Butterfield Grove. The original clubhouse was located in the back gardens of 101 and 103 Fairways, backing onto the Owendoher River.

Grange Golf Club, Taylor's Lane

In 1909, a small group of golf enthusiasts joined a new 9-hole golf club in Kilmashogue, which had just been laid out by Thomas O'Brien-Butler. They paid the owner a fee for playing, but had no say in the running of his club, so they decided to set up their own golf club, and leased enough land for a 9-hole course from the owner of Marlay Grange (a smaller house beside the north-east corner of Marlay Park demesne). They laid out the course over the winter of 1910/1911, and it was substantially ready for play by March 1911. Two months later, the timber-framed clubhouse opened, and this was extended on numerous occasions over the next ninety years, before being demolished in 2003, and a fantastic new clubhouse built.

By 1925, another nine holes had been laid out, this time on land leased from the new owner of Marlay demesne, the Love family. This family became very important to the club, because in 1933, the Loves bought the freehold of the inner nine holes from the owner of Marlay Grange, and then granted the club a 99-year lease of the entire 18 holes on 114 acres. Love sold the club the freehold of the entire course in 1967, just a few years before the

Marlay demesne was sold to Dublin County Council. When Marlay Grange was part sold in 1975, the club acquired an additional 45 acres, allowing them to boast of a 24-hole course.

Nowadays, we take for granted the beautiful landscape of this course, with manicured lawns, soft sandy bunkers, a wide variety of trees, the River Glin, etc, but we must not forget that the original farmland had to be laboriously shaped and excavated, trees and hedges cut down, and grass seed planted. In the early decades of the club's life, grazing sheep shared the space with intrepid golfers! Long before everyone had a car, the golfers had difficulty reaching this remote location, relying on some trams to Rathfarnham village, some White Line buses a little further, or the humble bicycle.

Golf clubs are sometimes assumed to cater only for the affluent, but some clubs also have sections for Artisans (generally men in skilled trades). Artisans Clubs originated in England in the 1880's and spread to Ireland a few decades later. The Artisans section in the Grange Gold Club was started in 1937 by local lads, generally former caddies or groundsmen, and operated from an old cottage on the grounds. In the late 1960's, they acquired a permanent clubhouse near the present main entrance from Taylors Lane, which was formerly the home of the Grange Golf Club Professional. This quaint green-painted building was extended in 1985, and upgraded in 2004.

From the start in 1910, ladies were admitted to the club as Associate Members, but not as full Members. However, in July 2002, equal-status legislation finally forced the men to allow women full recognition.

And what about the original Kilmashogue Golf Club? It closed in 1911, and was only re-opened in 1995 as part of St Columbas College, and is now thriving.

Castle Golf Club, Woodside Drive

In 1912, Bailey & Gibson, developers, purchased the Rathfarnham Castle demesne, comprising 290 acres, and the following year, they sold the castle itself and a small parcel of land to the Jesuit priests. Their intention was to build a housing estate and a golf course on the remainder of the estate. In 1913, they proceeded to lay out an 18-hole course, and build a clubhouse, on 100 acres, and reached an agreement with a group of golf enthusiasts to use the new course at set rates, except on Sundays. In the early days, sheep grazed on the course, and keep the grass tidy. 1914 saw the start of the First World War, and regulations required part of the course to be set aside for growing vegetables.

In 1917, members of the Castle Golf Club availed of the opportunity to purchase the golf course from Bailey & Gibson, for £8,250. By 1926, a new two-storey clubhouse had been erected, size 80 feet by 53 feet, which was to last until a major fire on Christmas Day 1970, after which a new clubhouse was completed in 1973. The present building is the result of an extension and major upgrading in 2001. The original course was also upgraded around this time, followed by the formation of a 6-hole, par 3, mini course around one of the former castle lakes in 2007.

From the inception of the club in 1913, women were allowed Associate membership, and it wasn't until 2001 that the law forced the men to allow women full equal rights.

The club formed an Artisans Section in 1950, for former caddies and maintenance staff. The Juvenile Section dates from the late 1960's.

The First World War put paid to the developers original plan to build a housing estate on part of the estate, and it wasn't until the 1980's that Castleside Estate and then Rathfarnham Wood were built.

Originally the course entrance was from Main Street, Rathfarnham, to the north of the former Castle gate lodge, not far from the tram terminus, but within a few years the gate lodge (Ely Arch) on Dodder Park Road was the main entrance, especially for motorists. The old pedestrian entrance gate was moved further east, and can still be seen right beside the Quaker Meeting House on Crannagh Road.

Edmondstown Golf Club, Edmondstown Road

The Dublin Maccabean Golfing Society was founded by a group of Jewish enthusiasts in 1933, and its members played in a variety of clubs, although were not allowed to join as full members. In 1943, the Society purchased a farm of 72 acres in Rathfarnham, called Edmondstown Park, and officially set up the Edmondstown Golf Club Ltd for members of the Jewish community. The first official meeting of the company was held in April 1944 in Zion Schools, Bloomfield Avenue, in Portobello. The house itself was not included in the sale, so the farmhouse outbuildings were used as the initial clubhouse, supplemented in 1953 by a Nissan hut, which came from the Arcadia Ballroom in Bray. The early Captains Dinners were held in the Greenville Hall, part of the synagogue on the South Circular Road (nearly opposite the National Stadium). In 1960, a new clubhouse was built, and this in turn was substantially rebuilt in the 1990's.

The golf club was associated with the Dublin Maccabi Association, which operated the Carlisle Cricket Club on Kimmage Road West (now a Ben Dunne Gym).

There was great excitement in 1950, when a Bronze-Age Flat Cemetery was discovered on the present 14th fairway, which cemetery is now a National Monument (DU022-029). A number of skeletons and burial chambers were un-earthed by archaelogists, including pottery and other objects.

The initial course was 9-hole, but extra holes were created over the years, so that by 1959, they had 18-holes. Nowadays, the club also has non-Jewish members. Lady Associates were permitted from the start, and were allowed full membership in 2004, under Equal Status legislation. There is also an Artisans

Section for local men, generally former caddies and greenkeepers, who can play at restricted times.

The course commands wonderful views of the Dublin Mountains, and across to Howth, and amidst the planted trees, the River Glin winds its way.

Ballinascorney Golf Club, Kilmashogue Lane
Started in 1971 in Bohernabreena, and moved to Rathfarnham (beside the entrance to St Columbas College) in 2002.

Stackstown Golf Club, Kellystown Road
Founded by the Gardai in 1976, behind the Taylors Three Rock pub, it now has 20 holes, and is open to non-Gardai.

The 9th green on the original Rathfarnham Golf Course, Butterfield Avenue, with clubhouse in the background, and Owendoher River behind. Left to right: Ms Chamney, Ms Malone, Ms Robertson, Ms Leary. (Courtesy of Rathfarnham Golf Club).

Sports Clubs

Three Rock Rovers Hockey Club, Grange Road

Three Rock Mountain lies south of Rathfarnham, and is notable for the large number of television and communication masts. No one knows why a men's hockey club chose this name, because when the Three Rock Rovers Hockey Club was founded in 1893, they were based in Leopardstown, some miles from the mountain. They are the second oldest hockey club in Ireland, only a few weeks after Trinity College Dublin founded a club. After a period in Foxrock, at the corner of Westminster Road and Torquay Road, they moved to Londonbridge Road, Irishtown, in 1930, sharing their premises with the Lansdowne Lawn Tennis Club, before moving to Grange Road in 1981, only a "stones throw" from the actual Three Rock Mountain. Their new home was the 11 acre former stables and indoor jumping arena attached to Marlay Grange. The club immediately demolished the equestrian centre, and built an impressive clubhouse, and an all-weather astro-turf pitch, although managed to retain an old two-storey groom's house for their caretaker.

Meanwhile, a woman's hockey club, Maids of the Mountain, had been founded in 1918, initially sharing accommodation in Foxrock with Three Rock Rovers Hockey Club, before acquiring their own premises (shared with other clubs) in Templeogue in 1934. In 1988, they moved to Grange Road, again sharing facilities with Three Rock Rovers, before fully amalgamating with them in 1999.

These days, the club has two all-weather and floodlit pitches (watered by supplies from their own 80 metre deep well), in addition to a grass football pitch at the rear (used until four years ago for cricket), the latter used by Stillorgan-Rathfarnham Rugby Football Club, and by the Dublin Rebels (American Football

Club). Many local schools also play soccer and Gaelic Football at the Grange Road pitches.

Ballyboden St Endas GAA Club, Firhouse Road

This famous GAA club, with its clubhouse on the Firhouse Road, was founded in 1969, with the amalgamation of three local clubs, Ballyboden Wanderers (founded in 1910), Rathfarnham St Endas (founded 1966), and St Josephs Boys Club. The first meeting was in Ballyroan Boys National School, under chairman Ned Murphy. The club premises are the original St Endas ground on the Firhouse Road, beside the former Leinster Hockey Ground. The club now has around fifteen pitches in different locations, and has the use of four school pitches. They have 140 teams, and 3,500 members. The six-week Summer Camps are very popular, as is their magazine, Boden News.

In 2001, the club bought 15 acres of the Santa Maria lands in Ballyroan from the Mercy Sisters, including the former convent house called "Ballyroan", and built an all-weather floodlit pitch, and a spare pitch. They share the facilities with the Santa Maria girls, including the changing rooms in the former TB Preventorium beside the old house.

Ballyboden Wanderers played their first match in the grounds of St Endas School, with the permission of the new occupier, Padraig Pearse. They disbanded in 1932, and reformed in 1961. In 1980 some old members reformed the club, and are still going strong in Frank Kelly Park, Mount Venus Road. There is a nice photo hanging in Revels pub in Main Street, showing the team of 1928.

Ballinteer St Johns, Grange Road

This newish GAA club was founded in 1982, and is now based in their 2003 clubhouse at the edge of Marlay Park, opposite Ballinteer Avenue.

Larch Hill Scouting, Mutton Lane, Pine Forest

John O'Neill occupied the house called Larch Hill, at a high altitude in a wooded area of the Dublin Mountains, in the early decades of the 19th century, using it as a Summer residence only. The two-storey house was three-bays wide, and four bays deep. An impressive white marble obelisk headstone on the family grave in the graveyard attached to Whitechurch church commemorates the family.

In 1906 the house was converted into a private TB hospital called Larch Hill Sanatorium, which operated until about 1920, after which it became Larch Hill Tea Rooms, favoured by hikers and mountaineers. TB was a dreaded disease in those days, and was also known as "Consumption". Dr Leopold Hare was the Chief Medical Superintendent at Larch Hill.

The old house and estate were bought by the Catholic Boy Scouts of Ireland in 1937, for use as camping and adventure weekends. The scouting movement now have their headquarters here, but the old house was demolished some years ago. The ancient "cromlech" in the grounds will be of interest to archaeologists.

13th Dublin Rathfarnham Unit (Scouts), Nutgrove Avenue

The unusual-looking tall plain building on Nutgrove Avenue was built in the 1970's as a Turf Depot, for those entitled to free fuel from the Government, but in 1986, it was converted into the Rathfarnham Scout Den, by inserting a concrete 1st floor, rear extension, etc. However, the scouts have been in Rathfarnham since 1943, occupying various temporary premises, often on only one evening a week. Their first den was in a terraced two-storey house, called Brooklawn, at the south end of Main Street. Then followed short periods in Fairbrook near the Tuning Fork pub, the old Courthouse on Main Street (not when the Court was sitting!), beside Hallmark Cards on Butterfield Avenue, Rathfarnham Workers Hall behind the Garda Station in the 1950's (the hall was nicknamed "The "Bluebird"), Nutgrove House (the White House beside their current premises, before it was demolished in the late 1960's), then in the Boys School on Willbrook Road.

Their present permanent home is very spacious and homely, and provides wonderful activities for young lads.

Three Rock Rovers Hockey Club, Silver Park, Leopardstown, 1893/94.
(Courtesy of Three Rock Rovers Hockey Club)

Maids of the Mountain Hockey Club, 1919/20. Rear, left to right: G. Mahony, V. Balfe, M. Balfe, P. Mahony, E. Keily, G. Eyre. Front: D. Pim, M. Lynch, H.O'Reilly, P. Roper, U. Minch. (Courtesy of Three Rock Rovers Hockey Club).

Maids of the Mountain Hockey Club, 1935. Standing, left to right: Rosamund Huet, Aileen Moore, Vera Mahony, Gwenda Robinson, Dorothy Lavery, Louise Hutton. Seated: Peggy Gamble, Mary O'Reilly, Patricia Thompson, A. N. Other, Nancy Leonard. (Courtesy of Three Rock Rovers Hockey Club).

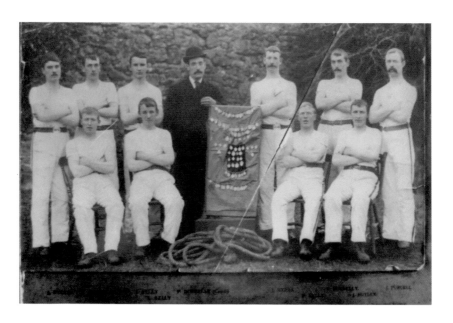

Whitechurch Tug-of-War team. (Courtesy of Seamus Kelly).

Rivers & Mills

Rathfarnham lies in the foothills of the Dublin Mountains, and the rainwater run-off is channelled into a variety of steep rivers and streams, which were used in the 18th and 19th century to provide motive power in many mills (factories), long before the ages of steam power and then electricity. Water naturally flows downhill, gathering speed and power, but mills were generally not positioned on the river. Instead, a weir or dam was built across the river, directing part of the river into a man-made channel, called a "head-race", which flowed into the mill water-wheel further down-stream, causing the wheel to rotate and power machinery, and then the water flowed back into the river further down-stream via a "tail race". Most mills had a big mill-pond, for the storage of water in Summer, and as a means of regulating the flow of water to the mill-wheel via sluices (vertical sliding wooden gates).

River Dodder

The River Dodder is a major Dublin river, rising at Kippure Mountain on the border of County Wicklow and County Dublin, and later flowing west to east as a division between Rathfarnham and Terenure, and fed only one local mill, Rathgar Mill, east of Rathfarnham/Pearse Bridge. Instead, a major tributary, the River Owendoher (and its own tributary, the Whitechurch Stream), supplied the water-wheels of around two dozen mills in the general Rathfarnham area.

Rathfarnham Bridge at the south end of Main Street passes over the Owendoher River (at a much lower level), and Pearse Bridge passes over the River Dodder in the valley between Terenure and Rathfarnham. The latter single-arch limestone bridge was built in 1765, and imaginatively named "The Big

Bridge", replacing earlier bridges (the earliest timber bridge was erected in about 1381). In 1952, the bridge was doubled in width, by building a reinforced concrete arch alongside the old stone bridge, and renaming it the Pearse Bridge, with a bronze plaque of Padraig and William Pearse.

Owendoher River

Rises in the Dublin Mountains as two separate streams, the Killakee Stream from the Killakee Mountain, and the Glendoo Stream from Cruagh Mountain, which merge near Edmondstown, runs alongside the Edmondstown Road and then Ballyboden Road, before eventually flowing into the River Dodder just west of Woodview Cottages, at the bottom of Church Lane.

Whitechurch Stream

Also known as the River Glin, it rises near Tibradden, flows through the Grange Golf Club, St Endas Park (Pearse Museum), alongside Whitechurch Road, before joining the Owendoher River at Willbrook Road, just past Fanagans Funeral Parlour (former Tuning Fork pub).

The Castle Stream

This rises in the vicinity of Barton Road, flows through Loreto Abbey and the west side of Castle Golf Club, before joining the River Dodder east of the Ely Arch.

The Little Dargle

Rises around Ticknock, flows through Marlay Park, and along the east side of the Castle Golf Club, before joining the Castle Stream, and flowing into the River Dodder near the Ely Arch.

"The Ponds"

In the early decades of the 19th century, "Lower Rathfarnham" centred on the Loreto Abbey, and comprised a maze of narrow lanes and cottages. The area was also known as "The Ponds", because there was a real pond in the centre, and in fact the pond can still be seen to the north of the former Loreto Abbey, directly behind the nun's new convent.

Ballyboden Waterworks, Stocking Lane

In the 1880's, the Rathmines Commissioners wanted their own water supply for the Township, instead of Dublin Corporation's supply. Their Dodder Water Supply Scheme comprised two holding reservoirs (lakes) at Bohernabreena (actually at Glenasmole), collecting water from the River Dodder, one lake of clear water for drinking purposes, and the other of peaty water destined for the mills along the Dodder. A pipe carried the clear water to a treatment works at Ballyboden, comprising filtration beds, and then a service reservoir of drinking water containing 54 million litres, which delivered the water into the public water mains in the surrounding suburbs. The treatment works were upgraded in recent years, doing away with the filtration beds (now a yard and carpark). In 2018, the old reservoir was abandoned, and a new covered reservoir built alongside, with a capacity of 16 million litres of water. Because of the health hazards from bird droppings etc, modern reservoirs need to be covered over.

The treatment building has a lovely Dublin Corporation logo over the entrance door, which roughly corresponds with the medieval city seal of 1230, showing archers defending the city against attack, and others blowing horns to alert the inhabitants.

Mills

Archer, writing in 1801, recorded one flour mill occupied by Newman, Curraghan, & Flanagan, a corn mill occupied by Drumgold, a paper mill occupied by Freeman, and another paper mill occupied by Teeling. There was a threshing mill owned by David La Touche in Marlay. Archer also recorded six paper mills in Rockbrook.

After examination of maps and directories from the 19th century, the following mills are identifiable.

Ely Mill, Rathfarnham Road

In the 18th and 19th centuries, there was a substantial mill beside the south-west corner of "The Big Bridge" (now called Pearse Bridge). The mill is listed on Frizells 1779 map as Widow Cliffords Mill, on 3½ acres, plus nearby house and garden.

The mill was powered from a millrace off the Owendoher River, starting high up on the west side of Rathfarnham village, although the "tail-race" flowed into the River Dodder.

Dalton, writing in 1838, said that the woollen mill was run by Murray, and employed 50 staff.

The Landed Estates Court sold the mill and Ashfield House in 1875. The 7-acre mill and demesne had a lease dated 1811, between the Marquis of Ely and Patrick Lambert, and at the date of sale was listed as Ely Flour Mill. By the 1880's the mill had been demolished.

Rathfarnham Paper Mill, Church Lane

In the 17th century, most paper was brown in colour, and for hundreds of years, paper was manufactured from cloth rags, pounded into a wet pulp, and pressing the mixture through very fine steel meshes.

In England, a group of mostly Huguenots (French Protestants) set up the "Company of White Papermakers", having been granted a Royal Charter by King James II in 1686. One of that group, Nicholas Dupin, based in Portsmouth, decided to expand to Ireland, and obtained a patent in 1690, and within two years had built a paper mill in Rathfarnham, west of the Main Street. It seems he was unsuccessful, and left in 1696. Following a fire, the mill was rebuilt in 1776. Other paper makers operated the mill for the next fifty years, including the Slators.

Frizells map of 1779 has a little sketch of the mill, including the water wheel. Shown as "old mill" on an 1843 OS map, and as flour mill on an 1864 OS map. The mill was derelict by 1912, and the charming Wood View Cottages built adjacent in 1916. Modern houses called "Rathfarnham Mill" have now been built on the site.

Sweetmans Flour Mill, Butterfield Avenue

For most of the 19th century, there was a mill, and a big mill-pond, at the south end of Main Street (beside the present Anne Devlin sculpture), which was marked on an 1801 map as the Manor Mill, presumably belonging to the Castle. It became known as Sweetmans Flour Mill, although there were different occupiers until it closed in 1887. The pond was filled in, and a garage was on the site for many recent years. Village Court apartments were built on the south side of the site in 1993. The Castle itself also had a Saw Mill beside their large pond.

Silveracres Mill, Whitechurch Road.

Not far from the former Tuning Fork pub (now Fanagans Funeral Parlour) there was an old mill, marked on an 1801 map as a paper mill run by Richard Freeman. Mark Flower operated a pin mill here in the period 1836-1853, and then other occupiers used it as a flour mill until about 1933. The mill itself has since been demolished, although the substantial manager's house is now back in residential use. Most of the single-storey mill-workers cottages to the north are now derelict.

Willbrook Flour Mill, Whitechurch Road
St Gatiens House was built on this old flour mill site, at the south-east of the present Ford Garage.

Alderman J. J. Kelly operated the National Tobacco Company in 1922, from Camden Street and 8 Harcourt Road. He had grown tobacco at St Gatiens in 1911/12 with greenhouses 80 yards long. His father had previously grown tobacco in Wexford.

In the 1930's and 1940's, the St Gatiens School of Gardening was in business here.

Ballyboden Mills
There were two mills in the vicinity of Bolton Hall to the north of Taylors Lane. On the east side was a paper mill, operated by Nicholas Ryan (and then Brown), while on the west side, adjoining Ballyboden Road, was a cloth mill operated by Reid. The Ryan paper mill had a water-wheel of 12 feet diameter, 6 feet 9 inch wide buckets on the wheel itself, and a fall of water of 12 feet 10 inches.

Around 1950, Ballyboden Crescent was built by the county council on the site of the cloth mill. The paper mill was demolished to make way for Glendower Close housing, but thankfully, Bolton Hall has recently been restored, despite a serious fire in the derelict house in 2009, and some of the outbuildings of the former paper mill have been converted to residences. Some distance to the north of these mills was a cloth mill (later a flour mill), which has disappeared, although a small house was built on the foundations, and a pleasant stream still flows through the substantial wooded grounds, called "The

Wood", or Ait an Cuian, with frontage to Ballyboden Road. The artist, Sean Keating, lived here in the 1950's.

Newbrook Paper Mill, Taylors Lane

Built in the 1750's, this paper mill was first operated by Mansergh, and then McDonough, residing in Newbrook House and Kingston House, and was one of the few in the locality which did not change to cloth or flour milling in the 19th century. In the 1840's there were two water-wheels. The wheel for bruising pulp was 16 feet diameter, with 4 feet 6 inch buckets, and a fall of water of 16 feet, providing 10 horse power (HP). The wheel for working the machinery was 14 feet diameter, with 1 feet 10 inch buckets, a fall of water of 13 feet 6 inches, providing 6 HP.

The last owner from 1899 was Sir John Irwin, J.P., a Presbyterian, who bought it in a derelict condition, and traded as S. Irwin & Son. He had another premises at 121 Upper Abbey Street, where young girls sorted loads of waste paper, which Irwin bought from premises around the city. In 1922, there was a fire at the Newbrook Mill, which was successfully dealt with by the Rathmines Fire Brigade. Irwin died in Newbrook House in 1935. Following a fire in the mill in 1942 it was demolished, but Newbrook House still stands, although empty for a long time. There was a Builders Merchants beside it until recently, called Merchant Meade.

Sherlocks Cotton Mill, Edmondstown Road

Just south of Billy's Bridge, there were two mills in the 19th century. The north one was Sherlocks Cotton Mill, which was later marked as a Fulling Mill on the 1864 OS map. The 1840's valuation recorded a Wash Mill and a Wadding Mill, a 15 feet waterwheel with 5 feet 4 inch buckets, and a 12 feet fall of water.

It operated as the Edmondstown Model Laundry from about 1875 to 1920, but from 1900 it was owned by the

Bloomfield Laundry, which was based at Willbrook Road (now Otterbrook housing estate).

Paper Company, Edmondstown Road

This paper mill was a short distance to the south of Sherlocks Mill, and was operated by Dollards from 1848 to 1896, who also operated the Millmount Mills further up the road around this period.

Reckitt & Sons, Edmondstown Road

In the early decades of the 19th century, John Reid operated a cloth mill beside the River Owendoher at the south end of this narrow roadside site, with workers cottages towards the north end. The Valuation Office House Books recorded a water-wheel of 20 feet diameter, 5 feet wide water buckets, a fall of 20 feet, and 4 to 5 revolutions a minute.

Reckitt & Sons, an English company, set up an Irish subsidiary in 1911, and immediately modified the existing mill for their needs, and demolished some cottages to make space for a new mass-concrete built factory alongside the road. Seemingly, they installed a water turbine in the original stone-built mill, to harness the river for electricity.

Company advertisements in the 1920's were for products such as Robin Starch (ironing shirt collars), No 4 Enameline Stove Polish (cooking range and fireplace grates), Brasso (polishing door knobs, and the "family silver"), Nilux, Rising Sun, Zebra, etc. In the 1930's, they were also making Steradent for cleaning dentures. In the 1940's, the increased range of products included Harpic Toilet Cleaner, and Dettol.

Reckitts went into partnership with J & J Colman in the 1940's, to form Reckitt & Colman, the latter making mustard on the same site. By the 1970's the company had works in Rathfarnham, Bluebell, and Castlebellingham. In 1986 they moved to Belgard Road, and sold Edmondstown Mill, which was used by Chemserve for some years.

This historic site was recently sold, and there is Planning Permission to convert the original stone buildings into apartments, and to provide additional residential accommodation elsewhere on the site, all a very welcome proposition.

Millmount, Edmondstown Road.

In 1843, Millmount was available for letting, having lately been occupied by Francis Pickering, paper manufacturer. Pickering seems to have been involved in a number of Rockbrook mills within the previous decades. A nearby mill was also for letting in 1843, having recently been occupied by Walter Mahon, cloth manufacturer.

Dollards had the paper mill at Millmount from around 1850 to 1900.

Brown had a paper mill around this time at nearby Newtown Great, which site is now Edmondstown National School, built in 1954 (the original old school was about 100 metres to the north, demolished to make way for the M50).

Millmount was situated nearly opposite The Merry Ploughboy pub, but the ruin was demolished in recent decades. A partial ruin (only a single-storey gable wall) of the former mill at Newtown Little, is nicely preserved nearby at Hole 9 on Rathfarnham Golf Course.

Rockbrook Mills, Edmondstown Road

Alongside the entrance driveway to Rockbrook Park School, are the substantial ruins of an 18th century paper mill, started in the 1770's, beside Rockbrook House (which is reputed to be a few decades older than the mills). In fact, there are remains of two mills, the Upper Mill and the much more substantial Lower Mill, the latter at the same level as the Glendoo branch of the Owendoher River.

The Freemans Journal newspaper reported in 1840 that this Fry property was for sale, comprising Rockbrook House, paper mills, and 46 acres, with 40-years of the lease unexpired. Three years later, the property was for sale again, this time as a cloth mill, including looms, tenters, carding machines, etc.

The owners of Rockbrook Park School are to be commended for doing their best to prevent the historic ruins from completely disappearing, by doing some repairs, capping tops of walls, etc.

There was an interesting piece about court cases listed in the Freemans Journal of 1803, reporting that Darby Murray was sentenced to be transported for life (presumably to Australia) for the crime of making Bank of Ireland paper at a paper mill in Rockbrook, although the exact mill was not specified.

Kilmashogue Mill

Near the present entrance to St Columbas College, there was a Woollen Mill still operating in the early decades of the 19th century, and run by Creighton in the 1840's according to the Valuation Office. This was powered by the Whitechurch Stream (River Glin).

Laundries

Prior to the invention of the domestic washing machine, most people hand-washed their clothes in the kitchen sink, using water and soap. Wealthier people sent some of their clothes to commercial laundries, especially shirt collars, table cloths, etc. Clothes could be dropped off at retail branches around the city, and some companies collected the soiled clothes from your house, and brought them back spotless. Laundries in the early days were located alongside rivers, in order to obtain free motive power, and as a source of water for the washing process. Sometimes they are listed as Wash Mills.

Bloomfield Laundry, Willbrook Road

This laundry was set up in 1898, beside the Owendoher River, and boasted of nine acres of bleach ground, and open-air drying (on clothes lines).

In 1922, they were listed as the Bloomfield Model Steam Laundry Company, with shops at 193 North King Street, 61 Talbot Street, 37 Upper Abbey Street, and 13 Harcourt Road. They also owned the Edmondstown Laundry around this time.

They were still trading in the 1960's, but the domestic washing machine was becoming cheaper and more popular, so by 1970, the empty premises was for sale, and Otterbrook housing estate was later built on the site.

Whitechurch Laundry, Whitechurch Road

The laundry started in 1830, to the south of the original Whitechurch Church and Graveyard. Lewis, writing in 1837, refers to Mr Bewley's bleaching grounds and laundry. The 1840's Valuation of Thomas Bewley's property recorded an 8 feet water-wheel for the mangling machine, with 3 feet wide buckets, and a fall of water of 8 feet. The wheel for drying the clothes was 10 feet diameter, with 3 feet buckets, and a fall of water of 9 feet.

In due course, the laundry passed into the hands of Thacker, and then Willoughby from 1903. A fire in July 1927 completely destroyed the factory and machinery, and the Rathmines Fire Brigade had to stand by helpless, because there was insufficient water from the adjoining Whitechurch Stream. However, the fire did not spread to Mr Willoughby house. Now the private house, Lissadell, occupies the site.

Nearby, north of the Moravian cemetery, there was a silk mill on a 1-acre site. When the Marley Demesne was sold by the Landed Estates Court in 1864, the former mill is shown on a map as being in ruins. At that stage, a Mathew Gahan, carpenter & builder, was in occupation, on a lease of 99-years from 1853, and he was prohibited from using the premises for manufacturing.

Edmondstown Model Steam Laundry, Edmondstown Road
Just south of St Augustine monastery, Sherlocks cotton mill was converted in 1873 into the Edmondstown Model Steam Laundry Company, which closed in 1920. The Bloomfield Laundry was involved in the company from 1900 onwards.

Hospital Laundry, Nutgrove Avenue
In the 1970's, the Hospital Joint Services Board ran a central laundry for all the Dublin Hospitals, and it was located beside the present Fire Station. Now there is a retail park on the site.

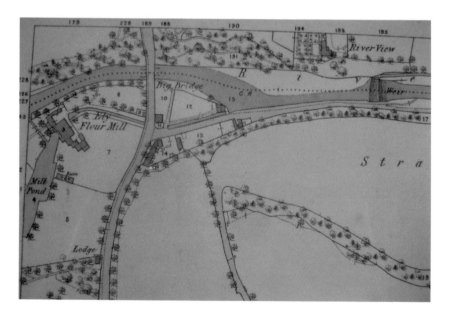

1864 Ordnance Survey map, showing the Ely Flour Mill beside the "Big Bridge" (now called Pearse Bridge). On the right-hand side, note the man-made weir on the River Dodder, which diverted part of the river into a "head race" alongside the north bank of the river, to power the Calico Printing Works a little further along at Waldrons Bridge (now called Orwell Bridge). (Courtesy of Trinity College Dublin Map Library).

Weir to east of Pearse Bridge, with the circular opening on the north bank, funnelling water into the "head-race" for the Calico Printing Mill at Orwell Bridge.

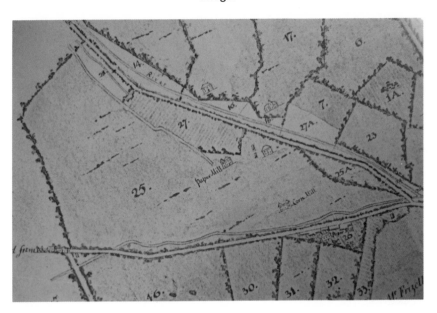

Byrnes 1801 map, with Ballyboden Road along the top, and Whitechurch Road along the bottom, with three mills, one corn (flour), and two paper.
(Courtesy of Trinity College Dublin Map Library).

1864 Ordnance Survey map of the Willbrook area, with Taylors Lane along the bottom, showing various mills/ponds. (Courtesy of South Dublin Libraries).

101

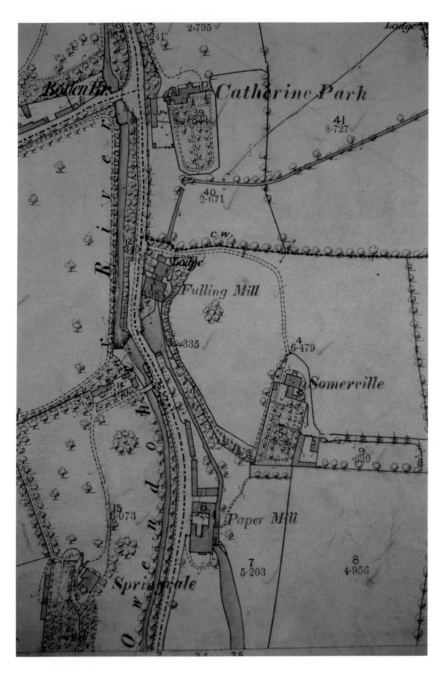

1864 Ordnance Survey map of Edmondstown Road near Taylors Lane. Boden Bridge is now nicknamed Billy's Bridge. (Courtesy of South Dublin Libraries).

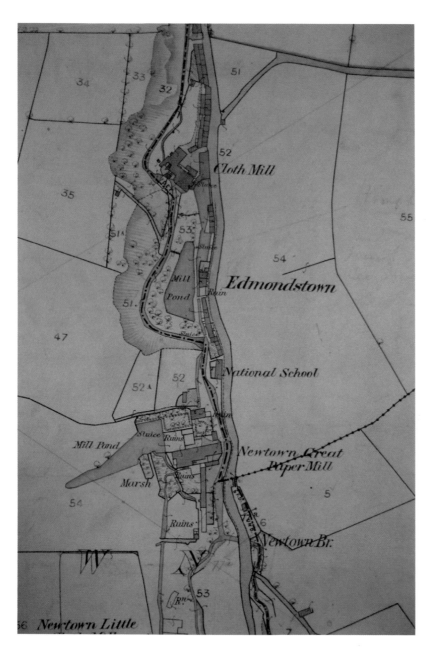

1864 Ordnance Survey map of Edmondstown Road, showing the Cloth Mill and extensive mill ponds at the top (later called Reckitts), and Newtown Great Paper Mill at the bottom (now Edmondstown National School). (Courtesy of Trinity College Dublin Map Library).

Former Reckitts on Edmondstown Road is still intact, and has planning permission for part conversion into residential accommodation.

The courtyard of former Reckitts, looking north. The concrete building on the right was built by Reckitts in 1911. The actual old stone mill is at the south end of the courtyard, partly at the level of the lower River Owendoher.

Artist's impression of the old mill, before Reckitts took over. (Courtesy of Seamus Kelly).

Looking north towards the original mill and pond used by Reckitts. (Courtesy of Seamus Kelly).

Lovely rural view looking south-west towards the Reckitts mill.
(Courtesy of Seamus Kelly).

Reckitts occupied an original stone mill building, which is still standing.
(Courtesy of Seamus Kelly).

Some of the old buildings before Reckitts took over. (Courtesy of Seamus Kelly).

The Edmondstown Supply Stores was the local grocery shop, before Reckitts became involved in the site. (Courtesy of Seamus Kelly).

Reckitts office staff. (Courtesy of Seamus Kelly).

Reckitts management team. (Courtesy of Seamus Kelly).

Reckitts employed a lot of women and young girls. (Courtesy of Seamus Kelly).

The entire Reckitts workforce and management. (Courtesy of Seamus Kelly).

The well preserved ruins of the Frys Paper Mill alongside the driveway of Rockbrook Park School.

The round tower "folly", in old Cruagh cemetery, Rockbrook. The original tiny chapel has now disappeared.

1864 Ordnance Survey map of Whitechurch Laundry. Note the original Whitechurch church in ruins at the top, and Graveyard. There is another small walled cemetery on the south side of the lane, backing on to the house "Palmyra". (Courtesy of Trinity College Dublin Map Library).

1916 letterhead for Bloomfield Laundry on Willbrook Road (now Otterbrook housing estate). (Courtesy of National Archives of Ireland).

The open reservoir of Ballyboden Waterworks has recently been superceded by a concrete-built covered reservoir.

Calico Printing Mill

This important mill deserves to be recorded, because it is was the only one in the locality powered by the River Dodder, via a mill race starting at the weir on the east side of Pearse Bridge. Calico was the term applied to plain white cotton fabric, but most people wanted to buy coloured (dyed) and patterned fabrics for dresses and other clothes.

The hockey pitches section of The High School beside Orwell Bridge was originally a Calico Printing Mill at the beginning of the 19th century (although the mill is reputed to have been on the site of another mill built in 1760). Taylors map of 1816 shows the "Rathgar Print Works". Samuel Lewis, writing in 1837, states: "There is an extensive bleach-green, with printing works belonging to Messrs. Waldron, Dodd, Carton, & Co., for muslin, calicoes, and silks: the works are set in motion by a steam engine of 30-horse power , and a water-wheel of equal force, and afford employment to 300 men. Lewis also records that a P. Waldron Esq. resides in a house called "Rathgar", presumably the same man who partly owns the mill. The 1837 Ordnance Survey map shows the mill, and adjoining house, "Rathgar". The map is very deceptive, since it does not show the cliff between the mill and the house, with the house on top and the mill at the same level as the adjoining River Dodder. However, the map does show the mill race, which is an artificial canal commencing upstream at a man-made weir just east of the Rathfarnham Bridge (Pearse Bridge), and running alongside the north bank of the River Dodder, widening-out in a long mill pond before reaching the mill. After running through the mill waterwheel, the water continues on for a short distance in a "tail-race", before re-joining the River Dodder just upstream of the Wooden Bridge (renamed Waldron's Bridge when Patrick Waldron built a single-arched stone bridge in 1848, and rebuilt in concrete as Orwell Bridge in the early 1970's). The mill had closed by the 1840's, but Patrick Waldron continued to reside in the house until the mid-1850's.

Laurence Waldron is listed in an Almanac for 1798 and 1803 as a wholesale linen draper, at 11 Inns Quay (Kings Inns Quay). In 1825, Waldron, Osbrey & Waldron, are listed as Calico Printers at 11 Inns Quay. They are still listed there in 1836, under the name, Waldron, Dodd, Carton & Co, in addition to having premises in Rathgar.

From 1846 to 1852, Patrick Waldron is listed as residing in Rathgar House, but the adjacent mill is not in use.

From 1858, William Carvill was residing in "Rathgar House", and operating the Carville Saw Mills from the former calico printing mill. Some of the old mill buildings were gone by now, leaving plenty of storage space. Carvill was a big timber importer, and had stores on Customs House Docks, where timber auctions were held. The Ordnance Survey map of 1864 also shows a quarry and lime kiln at the south end of the Rathgar site, presumably part of Carvills business (quarrying limestone, and reducing the stone by fire into lime powder in the kiln, for use by builders and farmers). After being disused for about ten years, by the mid-1880's, Rathgar Saw Mill was sub-let to Locke & Woods, who were also importers of timber (and slates from Wales), using George Bell as their shipping agent in Dublin. Newspaper advertisements in 1890 refer to a second store at 37, 38, 39 Sir John Rogersons Quay, and to their importation of Portland Cement from England. However, in 1894, Joseph Meade (a builder and alderman living in St Michaels, Merrion) petitioned the courts against William Hamilton Carvill, and Carvill's property was put up for sale. This included ground rents for the new houses on nearby Orwell Park, rentals for 1-14 Rostrevor Terrace, a house and land called "Orwell", Rathgar House (empty), and Saw Mill rented to Locke & Woods for £150 per annum. Locke & Woods remained in the Saw Mill until 1898, and then continued as timber importers at Sir John Rogersons Quay until 1902.

When Alderman Meade died in 1903, part of his estate was sold, including Rathgar Saw Mills and about 12 acres. However, a Mrs Coffey had some claim on the mill, which was only resolved in 1907 by Court order, after which Ernest Bewley was able to purchase the mill and land, and allow him to extend his main holding of "Danum". Bewley never used or leased the mill after that, and within a few years it was derelict.

When The High School purchased the Bewley estate in the 1950's, the site comprised the house, "Danum", with land around it, and also the lower fields comprising the former bleach green and mill. However, the sale excluded a long two-storey former mill building immediately at the base of the cliff, which is still occupied by a relative of the Bewley family as a distinctive residence called "The Barn". Their charming garden still has an open (but dry) stretch of the old mill-race, with nice stone sides. The Barn included the ruins of the former Saw Mill, and the latter was only demolished in the mid-1990's to make way for five townhouses, called Park View. Orwell Park had been laid out in 1950 by Dublin Corporation prior to the sale of Danum to the High School, but the old lime-kiln can still be seen at the south end of this public park.

The former house above the mill, "Rathgar House", is currently the Orwell Private, a Nursing Home. From 1934 to about 1972, the house was used as a Bethany Home, a Protestant-run Mother and Baby Home, whose deceased members were buried in Mount Jerome Cemetery in Harold's Cross, and where a large headstone with their names was recently erected by volunteers. However, some of the former outbuildings can still be seen as a quaint enclave of cottages at the eastern end of Rostrevor Road.

The High School
The High School was opened in 40 Harcourt Street, Dublin, on the 1st October, 1870, under the umbrella of The Erasmus Smith Schools Trust. Erasmus Smith was an English merchant, who

supplied Oliver Cromwell with oats, flour and cheese, for his troops in Ireland. He also was a financial backer of Cromwell's campaigns, and in return for his services, he received thousands of acres of confiscated land in Ireland. Using income from renting these lands, Smith set up an educational trust in 1657, and some of this money was used to fund Protestant Grammar Schools (Secondary Schools) in Drogheda, Galway, Tipperary, Ennis, and around 240 English Schools (National Schools) in remote parts of Ireland. The trust also set up The High School in Dublin, more as an intermediate or commercial school for boys, preparing them for Trinity College, the civil service, army service, colonial service, etc. The trust received a Royal Charter in 1669.

40 Harcourt was purchased from Dean Pakenham in 1869 for £4,000, and the famous "Clockroom", size 80 feet by 28 feet, was built alongside that same year. Various extensions were added over the years, and a Junior School was established in due course. In 1921, a World War 1 three-light memorial window was installed in the "Clockroom, made by W. McBride of Craftworkers Ltd. Belgrave Square park was used for sporting activities, being leased from a private owner from 1880, and purchased in 1897. The Iveagh Baths off Patrick Street was used by the school for swimming.

In 1954, the school purchased a 21-acre property in Rathgar, called Danum, for £21,000. This had been the Bewley home (of café fame) since 1904/05, when Ernest Bewley built the red-brick house (since demolished). The Bewleys were members of the Society of Friends (Quakers), and attended Churchtown Meeting House. The Bewleys kept a herd of Jersey dairy cows in Rathgar, and the new red-bricked cow parlours were very modern for that era. Up until 1922, the Bewleys had a big flock of prize hens. Ernest Bewley also had a farm in Clondalkin, where he reared Jersey cows, and prize pigs (boars). Ernest was a long-time member of the Royal Horticultural Society of Ireland, and used his extensive glasshouses in Rathgar to produce prize dahlias and chrysanthemums. The Ordnance Survey map of 1936 shows a boathouse and waterfall near the River Dodder, where an old quarry had filled up with water.

The High School wanted the land for their football pitches, and also used one floor of the house as the headmaster's residence, thus freeing up rooms in Harcourt Street for classrooms.

In the late-1960's, The High School decided to sell 40 Harcourt Street, and build a new school in Rathgar. The former Bewley house was demolished in 1969, and the headmaster moved into the adjoining 38 Zion Road. The new school was built by G & T Crampton Ltd, funded by a partial grant from the Government, and a long-term loan from the Representative Church Body (RCB). The school opened in September 1971. 40 Harcourt Street was sold in 1969 for £400,000 (part of the site was later developed as a Garda Regional Headquarters), and Dublin Corporation bought Belgrave Square park. The World War 1 memorial window from Harcourt Street was re-erected in the foyer of the new Rathgar school. The archives of the Erasmus Smith Trust are now safely stored (and some on display) in a section of the former cow parlour (by this stage extended and altered to modern standards).

While Protestant boys were being educated in Harcourt Street, Protestant girls were being educated nearby in a completely separate school, not associated with the Erasmus Smith Trust. The imposing St Matthias Church was on Adelaide Road, and its National School in 20 Hatch Street needed a larger building, so a new single-storey Schoolhouse was built in 1851 at the corner of Earlsfort Terrace and Adelaide Road, catering for boys and girls, with infants added in 1870. The boys section closed around 1898. In 1904, the school was re-organised as the Diocesan Intermediate & Commercial School for Girls, although younger girls and infants were included (Intermediate was the term used for Secondary Schools). The Parochial Hall was included in the school building. An additional storey was added to the single-storey school in 1960, and surprisingly, around this time, nearby St Matthias Church was demolished.

The Diocesan School merged with The High School in Rathgar in September 1974, and the old school was bought by Irish Life Assurance Company, who built an office block on the site, now called Davitt House. An extra rear wing was added to the Rathgar High School to cater for the larger number of classrooms required for a co-educational school. The Junior School closed in 1982. The present co-educational and non-denominational school has about 700 students.

Nowadays, The High School has marvellous outdoor sporting facilities, including a brand-new all-weather rugby pitch on the east side of the school (this was originally a sunken croquet lawn for the Bewley family). Not visible to the casual observer is the steeply-sloping path at the south-east of the rugby pitch, which leads down to another part of the campus, where there are two modern hockey pitches for the ladies, and older tennis courts, all at one time the site of the Calico Printing Mill and bleach field. These facilities can also be accessed from a formal entrance on Orwell Road.

Marianella, Orwell Road

In 1910, the Redemptorist priests bought 30 Highfield Road for use as a novitiate, and named it "Marianella". Soon, larger premises were needed, and the priests bought "Faunagh House, 75 Orwell Road in 1919, and re-named it "Marianella".

In 1968, a modern monastery was built on the same site, and the period property demolished. A circular chapel was added to the rear in 1974, which was open to locals for Mass.

In recent decades, the priests sublet space beside the south end of their monastery for a Driving Test Centre, and a Fitness Gym was built alongside.

The entire site was sold a few years ago, and blocks of luxury apartments have recently been built.

1843 Ordnance Survey map of Rathgar Calico Printing Factory and Rathgar House at Wooden Bridge, later called Waldrons Bridge, and now Orwell Bridge. The other Rathgar House at the top was demolished to make way for Oaklands, which became St Luke's Hospital. (Courtesy of South Dublin Libraries).

119

By the 1860's, the Rathgar Calico Printing Factory had been converted into a Saw Mill, and the other buildings demolished. Note the "tail race" into the River Dodder. (Courtesy of Trinity College Dublin Map Library).

View from The High School tennis courts. The long building is a private residence, but was originally part of the Rathgar Calico Printing Works. Rathgar Nursing Home is to the rear, and at a much higher level.

Painting of The High School in Harcourt Street, with the Clockroom on left. Now the site of Garda Headquarters. (Courtesy of The High School, Rathgar).

Study Hall in Harcourt Street. (Courtesy of The High School, Rathgar).

1896 photo of Hockey team. (Courtesy of The High School, Rathgar).

Diocesan Secondary School for Girls, corner of Earlsfort Terrace and Adelaide Road. Now an office block. (Courtesy of The High School, Rathgar).

1968 Redemptorists monastery on Orwell Road, still unfinished, and the old "Marianella House" at rear awaiting demolition. Blocks of apartments have recently been built on the cleared site. (Courtesy of Redemptorist Archives).

Business

Rathfarnham Bakery, Main Street

John Landy, a native of Skerries, County Dublin, started in the Rathfarnham Bakery on Main Street in 1892, although there may have been a bakery of the same name previously on this site, since Garrett McDonnell are listed as occupying the Rathfarnham Bakery as far back as 1835. The premises comprised a shop outlet on the Main Street, with a large bakery building alongside. There was a fire in Landys Bakery in 1926, during a labour dispute, but no major damage was caused. By 1954 the premises was too small, and the company built a spacious bakery on Knocklyon Road, not far from the west end of Butterfield Avenue, but still retained the retail shop in Rathfarmham village until 1962, when they sold it to J. C. Walsh & Sons Ltd, manufacturers of Rosary Beads. Centra supermarket currently occupy the former retail bakery shop, beside Walsh's factory.

The wholesale bakery continued in Knocklyon Road until 1968, when the business closed. The Landys then let the bakery to Comans, who used it for many years as a bottling plant. Now Hersilwood housing estate sits on the site, behind the Applegreen petrol station.

J.C Walsh & Sons Ltd., Main Street

Thomas Haycock opened the Terenure Garage in Terenure Place in 1945. In December of that year, he founded Irish Consolidated Bead Company, in a small building on the garage site, which manufactured Rosary Beads, which were a very popular accessory for every Catholic. His main competitor at the time was Alex Mitchell.

In 1962, they bought Landys Bakery on the Main Street in Rathfarnham, in order to cope with the expansion of the business.

The rear bakery was demolished, and replaced by the present factory that same year (the original Landys shop is now the present Centra Supermarket). A showroom was built at that time, but replaced by the present gift shop in 1987. In those early days, there were around 70 workers employed. Landys rear stables are still in use as workshops etc by Walsh.

The company bought their own Connemara Marble quarry in 1983, located at Lissoughter, Recess, County Galway, and the marble is cut, crafted and polished in the Rathfarnham factory. These days, rosary beads are only one of many products made, and their shop in Rathjfarnham is full of wonderful jewellery, gifts and souvenirs.

Lamb Bros Fruit Farm, Nutgrove Avenue

Charles Benjamin Lamb, a Quaker, was born in England in 1864, and in 1886 (at the age of 22) he started jam-making at Fruitfield, Richhill, a small village between Armagh and Portadown, in the north of Ireland. He married Charlotte the following year, and went on to have four sons and two daughters. The 1911 census records a 1st class house with seventeen rooms, and many outbuildings including a School Room and a Mission Room.

In 1918, he expanded the business to Dublin, naming it Lamb Bros (Dublin) Ltd, using the trade name "Fruitfield", with the newly-built jam factory based at the Inchicore end of the Naas Road. He started the fruit farm on 100 acres of land in the Nutgrove area of Rathfarnham, around an old house called Prospect Farm, which later changed its name to Holylands House. Up until the 1950's, Nutgrove Avenue ended at Nutgrove House (the former boarding school, and later called the White House). In due course, he had other farms at Donabate (bought 1934), Malahide, and Athy in County Kildare. The 450 acre farm at Barley Hill, Athy in County Kildare, was also famous for its herd of 100 pedigree dairy shorthorn cattle, which won many prizes at competitions. The company boasted that the cow dung made great fertilizer for the fruit bushes and trees. This farm also had 400 pigs. In addition, the company bought fruit from private farmers. Every year, hordes of young people spent their Summer holidays picking fruit on the Lamb Bros farms, and in the mid-1950's, the company recorded over 2,000 girls in casual labour, picking strawberries, raspberries, blackcurrents, gooseberries, apples, plums, etc.

The company made the famous "Fruitfield Old Time Irish Marmalade", various jams and preserves, Terry's LK thick sauce, canned and bottled fruits, etc. During the Second World War, with all its shortages, shop customers had to bring along an empty jam jar, if they wanted to buy another pot of jam.

Charles Lamb died in 1944 and was buried in the Friends Burial Ground, Richhill, County Armagh. In due course, his son, Wilfrid Harris Lamb, who was a fruit and potato merchant in the Dublin Corporation Fruit Market (W.H. Lamb & Co Ltd), became chairman of the Lamb Bros business.

Fruitfield began to change during the 1970's, resulting in some redundancies, and the company later merged with Jacobs Biscuits. Fruitfield is now part of the Valeo group, with all production in England.

The fruit farm in Rathfarnham was developed as Loreto Park/Nutgrove local authority housing in the 1950's, and then Mountain View/Holylands local authority housing in the 1970's, followed by the Nutgrove Shopping Centre in 1984. Mountain View estate was named after an old house halfway up Beaumont Avenue (previously called Nowlan Avenue).

In 1977, Fontstown House fruit farm, on 180 acres, north-east of Athy, County Kildare, was sold (80 acres of fruit, and 90 acres of grass and grain). In 1982, Barley Hill Farm, on 198 acres, at Moone, east of Athy, was sold. That same year, the 254-acre Beaverstown Farm, at Donabate, County Dublin, was sold, and in 1985, 140 acres of that farm was acquired for the new Beaverstown Golf Club (which still boasts 36 acres of orchards scattered throughout the course).

HB Hughes Bros dairy, Whitehall Road/Nutgrove Avenue

A farmhouse called Hazelbrook was built by the Hughes family in the 1890's, and within a few years they began selling the milk from their herd of cows to the public, using the trade name Hughes Bros, initially doling our jugs of milk from a collection of churns, going about the parish by pony and cart. Decades later, milk bottles were introduced, and empty bottles from the previous day had to be left outside your hall door at night, because the milkman delivered around dawn. Hughes Bros were bottling milk in the early 1940's, and built a new Rathfarnham factory in 1946/48. In the 1960's, slow electric vans delivered the bottles of milk to households, instead of pony and cart.

Meanwhile, in 1926, Hughes Bros started another division of the business, namely HB Ice Cream, which became enormously successful.

In 1964, Hughes Bros was taken over by an American company, W.R. Grace.

In 1968, a competitor, Premier Dairies, took over the bottled milk division of Hughes Bros, in exchange for Premiers ice-cream division, and thereafter, Hughes Bros concentrated on ice-cream only.

From 1973 to 2003, Hughes Bros was owned by Unilever, after which the Rathfarnham factory closed down, with the loss of 175 jobs, although "HB Ice Cream" continued to be made by Lakelands Dairy in Cavan.

The factory site in Rathfarnham was soon afterwards developed as a retail park (Costa, Homebase, Harvey Norman), with houses and apartments to the rear.

Hallmark Greeting Cards, Butterfield Avenue

The Irish branch of this famous American company (with regional office in Middlesex, England) started in 76 Bannow Road, Cabra in 1958, before moving to a purpose-built factory on Butterfield Avenue in 1963, where they remained until 2000, extending the factory in 1978. In 1972, there were 210 employees, rising to 276 twenty years later, at which stage they could produce 250 million greeting cards per year, all for export. They were taken over by Wace in 1995, and then by Burgess a few years later, and when they closed in 2000, there were 140 redundancies. A developer immediately built Charleville Square, a mixture of houses and apartments. The Hallmark symbol was a black royal crown.

Preston & Hadfields, Church Lane
This varnish, stain, and enamel factory opened in Rathfarnham in 1926, and was known as the Presfield Works, behind the present AIB Bank on Main Street. In 1968, they became agents for Rentokill Water Repellent. The premises was for sale in 1970, after being taken over the previous year by the Macpherson Group. Included in the sale was the Tourville site behind the Anglican church, which was developed as an estate of town houses in the mid-1980's.

Glaxo Laboratories, Grange Road
This pharmaceutical company was on Grange Road since 1972, although the entrance was on Stone Masons Way. Later the company was known as Glaxo Smith Kline (GSK). The premises recently became the headquarters of Cement Roadstone Holdings (CRH), behind Lidl supermarket.

Youngs Caravans, Dodder Park Road
Many people will no doubt have fond memories of Youngs Caravans on Dodder Park Road, in the days before cheap package holidays to Spain. People took their holidays in Ireland, sometimes touring the highways and byways, pulling a caravan behind their car. Young had a great display of caravans, from small to big expensive models, laid out on a long strip of lawn, which could be bought outright, or rented. In 1991, the 10-acre site was sold to a developer for houses, now called "Woodside".

South end of Main Street. Landy's Bakery was through the archway on the left, and the retail shop fronted on to the street. (Courtesy of Anglican Church, Main Street, Rathfarnham).

Looking up Butterfield Avenue towards Main Street. Sweetmans Mill and Pond was originally behind the Landy's advertisement. (Courtesy of Anglican Church, Main Street, Rathfarnham).

South end of Main Street in 1968. Sweetmans mill and pond was on the site of Rathfarnham Garage. (Courtesy of Dublin City Library & Archive).

Front office wing of the former Landy's Bakery on Knocklyon Road, which was later occupied by Comans Bottling Plant, and is now Hersilwood housing estate.

1960's aerial view of Premier Dairies/HB Ice Cream, with Whitehall Road on the left, and Nutgrove Avenue along bottom. (Courtesy of Loreto Community Centre).

Bottled milk delivery float and horse, in Sarah Curran Avenue.
(Courtesy of Seamus Kelly).

Shops and Pubs

The Rathfarnham Golf Club leased the long strip of land between the north side of Butterfield Avenue and the River Dodder, and when they moved to Woodtown in the 1960's, a housing estate called "Fairways" (very original!) was developed, in addition to the long Rathfarnham Shopping Centre, which was opened by hotelier, Pascal Vincent Doyle, in 1969. H. Williams grocery supermarket was located where Penneys clothes supermarket is now, and Quinnsworth food supermarket was in the present Tesco food supermarket. There are also thirty smaller shops, a small branch of Bank of Ireland, in addition to an Oratory upstairs run by the Servite priests. However, there is no Post Office.

This big shopping centre changed life on the Main Street, but there are still a few shops left. Cosgrave Butchers (established in 1940) beside the present Centra (which was originally Landys Bakery Shop) formerly had an abattoir for slaughtering cows immediately behind their shop, and a holding yard further back. Nowadays the former abattoir is occupied by Expert Cycles. Rowans is a popular deli and off-licence at 12 Main Street, and was originally called Clarkes Stores in the 1950's.

Revels pub at 37 Main Street was previously called City House, run by Patrick McDonald. Custis was a pub/grocery at 39 Main Street in the first half of the-20th century, then Donnellan pub, and now The Castle Inn. "The Captains" was another pub at 19 Main Street in the 1970's, then rebuilt back from the road and called The Rathfarnham Inn, and finally called "The Sarah Curran" pub, before being turned into the present big crèche with car park in front.

The Yellow House pub has been a noted landmark for nearly two centuries, partly because it was positioned at the start of the route up to the Dublin Mountains for hikers, cyclists, motor-cyclists, and cars. A map for 1801 shows a "Yellow House" on the present site of the Church of the Annunciation, and an article in the Freemans Journal newspaper that same year suggests a country hostelry serving food. The present large building opposite the church was built in 1827, which was a brave enterprise, because this pub was practically out in the middle of the countryside. Originally the building was rectangular, but has been extended in length by building a new staircase, and also extended very much to the rear, and the front was obviously re-faced with yellow brick, possibly in the late 19th century. The Fair Green was originally behind this pub.

When the Yellow House was sold in 1910 as a pub cum shop, the auctioneers advertisement referred to two lavatories adjoining the shop, one bar parlour, two stores (one with loft overhead), bottling store, refreshment garden, with four summerhouses, etc. The residence overhead comprised hall and corridor, two large drawingrooms with folding doors, large diningroom, seven bedrooms, one W.C., bathroom (hot & cold), kitchen with close range, two pantries. The out-offices comprised stabling for four horses, coachhouse, harness room, two fowlhouses, piggery, coal store, etc. There was a well laid-out fruit and vegetable garden. Mr P. Walker purchased the Yellow House in 1910, and sold his dairy farm in Willbrook that same year, including stock of 70 cows (including 40 freshly-calved milch cows), 20 prime fat cattle (the remainder Strippers & Springers), 2 yearlings, 6 good working horses, batch of pigs (about 12 stone each), about 18 tons of First and Second Crop hay, 2 Spring grain carts (almost new), 4 milk carts, 1 field cart, 1 van, I new double-handled turnip pulper, milk cans, buckets, barrels, barrows, etc.

There was a pub at the intersection of Willbrook, Ballyboden, and Whitechurch Road, not surprisingly called the Tuning Fork. The pub closed years ago and lay vacant, until it was demolished in 2018, and Fanagans Funeral Parlour built on the large site, just in time for their bi-centenary celebrations in 2019. Further along, Ballyboden House is a long established pub, re-named Buglers when a new owner took over in 1954.

The "Furry Bog" in Whitechurch Green was opened in 1985, beside the Augustinian church, catering for this modern estate.

A few miles further up the Edmondstown Road, The Merry Ploughboy pub is a long established "watering hole", reputed to date from 1789. In recent decades, it was called O'Dwyers, and then Allens. After a change of ownership about ten years ago, the pub is now geared towards Irish cabaret for tourists, and also funeral parties attending numerous small local cemeteries.

In the Marlay Park locality, The Eden pub on Grange Road occupies a charming mid-18th century house.

The modern Taylor Three Rock pub near the south-east corner of Marlay Park on Kellystown Road, was the site of a small farmhouse called Harolds Grange (not to be confused with the original Harold's Grange, which was centred on the old house in Marlay Park), which was occupied by the Taylor family for most of the 20th century, and is now a huge thatched pub providing Irish cabaret for tourists. This building is in the townland of Taylor's Grange, but the farmhouse is marked as "Harold's Grange" on both the 1837 and 1907 Ordnance Survey maps. Anyone can apply a name to their own property, and frequently, houses with the same or similar names can be found in street directories and on old maps. In 1972, the Taylor family demolished their old farmhouse and built the Taylors Grange Hotel, which was advertising Bed & Breakfast for £2.25 a night, and the presence of the No 47 bus terminus outside (a single-decker bus). The hotel became very popular for cabaret and dinner-dances, and for The Peppermint Tree Night Club & Disco, which later changed its name to Le Butterfly. In recent years the premises changed hands, and was rebuilt in its present thatched form, catering for tourists seeking Irish cabaret.

The single-storey Old Orchard Inn on Butterfield Avenue was purpose-built in 1962, and has been extensively extended on all sides in the following decades.

The Tuning Fork pub was demolished in 2018, and Fanagans have built a Funeral Parlour.

The Tuning Fork pub in the days when Willbrook was a village in its own right. Here Cullen is the owner of Willbrook Tavern. (Courtesy of Seamus Kelly).

Ballyboden Post Office & Grocery near the corner with Taylors Lane. Christine Caffrey on left, Phyllis Kelly on right. (Courtesy of Seamus Kelly).

The homely Servite oratory upstairs in Rathfarnham Shopping Centre is an oasis of peace for weary shoppers, and there is daily afternoon Mass.

Taylors Grange Hotel was built in 1972 on the site of the Taylor farmhouse, and now there is a big thatched pub called Taylors Three Rock, with cabaret for tourists. (Courtesy of Tom Taylor).

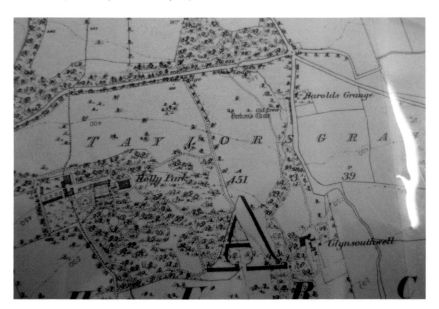

Taylors Three Rock pub was built on the site of a farmhouse called "Harold's Grange", as shown on this 1843 Ordnance Survey map. However, the townland was called "Taylors Grange". Holly Park is now St Columba's College, and Glynsouthwell is now Danesmoate. (Courtesy of South Dublin Libraries).

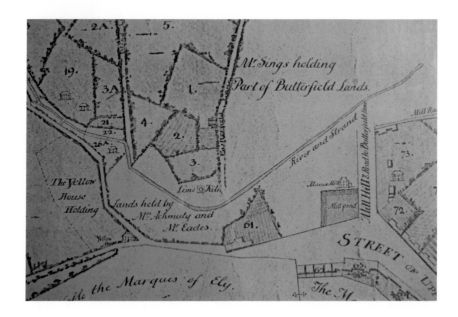

Byrne's 1801 map of Rathfarnham, showing the "Yellow House" on the site of the present Church of the Annunciation. Note the chapel house on Willbrook Road (plot 26A), and the "Manor Mill" and Mill Pond (also known as Sweetmans Mill) at the south end of Main Street. (Courtesy of Trinity College Dublin Map Library).

Law & Order

Military Road

Following the 1798 Rebellion, the British army built a road across the Dublin and Wicklow mountains to gain access to rebel hideouts. The project started in 1800, and was completed by 1809, including army barracks at Glencree, Laragh, Glenmalure and Aghavanagh. Glencree later became the notorious St Kevins Reformatory, and is now the Glencree Reconciliation Centre. These days, the road is called the R115, and starts at the Yellow House pub, up through Ballyboden, Stocking Lane, past the Hell Fire Club, and across the bleak barren landscape towards the Sally Gap, and onwards.

Courthouse

Rathfarnham had a Petty Sessions Courthouse from at least 1835, and it operated in much the same way as present-day District Courts, hearing criminal and civil cases. Around 1910 it was located at 3 Castle View, just to the north of the present AIB Bank.

A new Courthouse was built in 1912 on waste ground near the north end of Main Street. After the historic Boys school on Willbrook Road finally closed in 1977, the prestigious building was converted into a District Court, and the old one on Main Street was closed. In 2000, the Court was transferred to a new premises in Tallaght.

The Willbrook building reverted to the Church of the Annunciation, and in 2001 it re-opened as a Community Centre, after extending the 1915 brick-built school addition, and providing a pitched-roof. The 1912 Courthouse on Main Street is now used by a local athletics club.

Police

The un-armed Dublin Metropolitan Police (DMP) only operated within the city limits, and the armed Irish Constabulary controlled rural areas, including Rathfarnham. Their name changed to the Royal Irish Constabulary (RIC) in 1867. In 1922, the Garda Siochana (Civic Guards) was formed, and the DMP joined them in 1925. Because of some misconceptions concerning the role of the DMP and RIC before Independence in 1922, former members of both bodies were not enlisted in the new Garda Siochana, and some had no alternative but the join the Royal Ulster Constabulary (RUC) in the new Northern Ireland, whilst others faced unemployment, alternative occupations, or emigration. Contrary to popular belief, most policemen in the 19th century and the opening decades of the 20th century were Catholics, and Irish to the core, whilst only the very top positions were held by Protestants or Englishmen (or both), with varying political allegiances.

Rathfarnham village had a Police Station from at least 1835, and it was located just north of the present St Marys Terrace (north of the Yellow House pub). In the 1840's Valuation, the building was recorded as being 42 feet wide, 20 feet deep, and 18 feet high (probably two storey). By the turn of the century, it had moved to 16 Grange Road (later called Leighton Lodge), opposite the present entrance to Beaufort Downs housing estate. The 1901 Census recorded a sergeant (Catholic) and four constables (including one Protestant). In the 1911 Census, the sergeant was Protestant, and the four constables were Catholic.

The RIC leased an attractive 20-year old shop on Main Street/Church Lane for seven years from 1918, being two-storey at the front, and three-storey at the rear. The new Civic Guard was in occupation following the Treaty of 1922. At 9.00pm on the 11th January, 1923 (during the Civil War), the Civic Guard surrendered peacefully to armed men, who then placed a bomb/landmine, and blew up the front part of the premises. Neighbours had been ordered to vacate their shops, and their buildings only suffered minor damage. The shop owner, Robert McGrath, received £2,200 in compensation, and it was rebuilt by 1931, with an additional storey to the front section. The building was leased in 1932 to the Munster & Leinster Bank, who are still there, trading as AIB Bank.

The Garda Siochana seem to have occupied temporary premises, including 2 Castle View, a few doors away from their old premises at the corner of Church Lane, until new premises was built for them on Butterfield Avenue in 1938, including a Married Quarters block at the front, and they are still there today.

There was also a Police Barracks at Rockbrook, from around 1860, with gable wall to the road, thereby commanding views of the mountain road in both directions. The building is now a private house. In the 1901 Census, there was a sergeant (Catholic) and 4 constables (one Protestant). In the 1911 Census, there was a sergeant and three constables, all Catholic.

Property Damage, 1919-1923

During the War of Independence, 1919 to 1921, and the Civil War (1922-1923), various premises in Rathfarnham suffered some financial loss, but were compensated by the new Irish Free State. Examples include, William Willoughby of the Whitechurch Laundry (whose van driver was robbed of cash), James Mallen of Bloomfield Laundry (whose shop window at 128 Thomas Street was smashed), Patrick Walker in the Yellow House (soldiers commandeered his pub and used his food), J. Irwin & Son of Newbrook House paper mill (the "Irregulars" were in occupation of the RIC barracks on Main Street for some months during 1922, and took John Irwin's parked car to use as a barricade on Church Lane), etc. Edward Winder of Tourville, at the west end of Church Lane, also made a claim, since his antique furniture was taken by the "Irregular Troops", to barricade the Lane. John Landy operated Rathfarnham Bakery, Rathfarnham Motor Company, and Rathfarnham Coal Company, and he was targeted for lorries, and bread. Whitechurch Vicarage (formerly called Ormond) on Grange Road (now lost to Grange Wood housing estate), was burgled at least eight times, in failed attempts to gain entry and set fire to the building.

In 1924, The British Legion, a social club for former British soldiers, built a timber-framed clubhouse, 36 feet by 18 feet, on the Whitechurch Road, about 1½ miles from Rathfarnham village, and this was burned to the ground on the night of the 11th November, 1934.

Preston & Hadfield were paint and varnish manufacturers on Church Lane in the 1930's. In 1936, a collection of live bullets was found when they opened a cask of clay (used as a filler in paint), after it had been shipped from their supplier in Bristol, England. No harm was done.

RIC barracks at north end of Main Street and corner of Church Lane on 29th June, 1922. (Courtesy of Kilmainham Gaol Museum – Ref 2OPO-1A35-02).

Rathfarnham Gardai around 1950. (Courtesy of Seamus Kelly).

Old Houses

Marlay Grange, Grange Road/Taylors Lane
This small estate is closely linked with the history of Marlay Park, Grange Golf Club, and Three Rock Rovers Hockey Club.

The attractive house was built around 1874, when the north-east portion of Marlay Demesne was sold by the Tedcastle family. The Grange Golf Club acquired its course in stages, partly from the estate of Marlay Grange. But even when Marlay Grange was for sale in 1962, it comprised 125 acres, including a Stud Farm and an Equestrian Centre. By 1975, Marlay Grange was for sale again, this time only 61 acres and the Equestrian Centre. In 1978, the Equestrian Centre alone, on 11 acres, including 20 loose boxes, and an indoor Riding Arena, was for sale, which was acquired in 1981 by Three Rock Rovers Hockey Club.

Marlay Grange (comprising 12 acres at that time) was badly damaged by a malicious fire in 2010, but has since been restored by the private owner.

Silveracre, Sarah Curran Avenue
Silveracre, previously called Silverton, is an early 19th century house, with a substantial rear extension. It was probably built for the owner of the Silveracre Mill on adjacent Whitechurch Road (near Fanagans Funeral Parlour). The building was recently restored and divided into two houses, and six big houses built in the leafy grounds.

Butterfield House, Butterfield Avenue
This late-Georgian house, with unusual mansard-style roof, has its attractive back to the main road, and the front is rarely seen by the public. John Healy Hutchinson is the most famous name

associated with the house, which is nowadays used by the Irish Pharmacy Union as their headquarters.

Orchardstown House, Butterfield Avenue
Situated behind Washington House, Orchardstown House was a private lunatic asylum, run by W. S. Stanley from 1858 to 1892. Now in private ownership.

Ashfield House, Brookvale Road/Rathfarnham Road
This big house is shown on Frizell map of 1779, and Samuel Lewis also refers to it in 1837. Old deeds refer to it as Cherry Tree House. The Tottenham family lived here in the 19th century, and then the Brooks family (of Brooks Thomas, Builders Providers) in the 20th century, when the Terenure & District Horticultural Society staged their annual show in the grounds. The house is now in office use, surrounded by a modern housing estate.

Riversdale, beside Boden Wood, Ballyboden Road
The famous poet and playwright, William Butler Yeats, leased this house, alongside the Owendoher River, from 1932 1939, but he was in France when he died in 1939. He was buried in France, but ten years later some of his bones (supposedly) were taken from the communal ossuary, and buried in a churchyard at Drumcliff in County Sligo. Riversdale House is now in office use, surrounded by a few modern houses. His father, the famous artist John Butler Yeats, lived in 418 Harolds Cross Road (listed as 10 Ashfield Terrace in those days) from 1883 to 1887.

Washington Lodge, Grange Road
Directly opposite Beaufort High School, there are a collection of old 18th century houses, which at one time had fashionable occupants. Starting at the lane just past Loreto Abbey, is Abbey

View, followed by a showroom for heating stoves. No 26 is next, and then a block of modern apartments on the corner of a lane, where Snugborough was demolished. On the other corner of the lane is Washington Lodge. Behind this collection of buildings, there is a small industrial estate, occupying barn-like buildings with red corrugated roofs. On the other side of the road, the quaint St Patricks Cottages were built by the council in 1916.

Danesmoate, Kellystown Road

Originally called Glynsouthwell, and now in private ownership. The lease goes back to 1763 between Thomas Taylor and Richard Thwaites, when it was part of Holly Park (now St Columbas College). This charming estate has a small waterfall at the south end, on the Little Dargle River. The ancient "Brehons Chair" (three upright granite stones, about 8 feet high) was once a feature of the grounds, but is now in the modern adjacent housing estate of the same name.

Ely Lodge, Nutgrove Avenue

Ely Lodge, a late Georgian house, is still in use for a few small enterprises. The building backs on to the Castle Golf Club, and there are narrow carparks and garage workshops on both sides.

Health

Dispensary, Loreto Lane

The dispensary was regarded a mini public hospital, where people could obtain free medical advice, free medicine, etc. The one in Rathfarnham was established in 1801 on Willbrook Road, just south of the old chapel. In the 1840's, the Valuation Office recorded it as being 15 feet wide, 14 feet deep, and 7 feet high. In the early days, dispensaries were established by the Poor Law Guardians, and Rathfarnham was governed by the South Dublin Union. By 1860, the dispensary had moved to its present location, and was rebuilt as a bungalow in the mid-20th century, extended in 1969, and is nowadays called the Rathfarnham Health Centre. Every baby has to be vaccinated against various diseases in their local Health Centre. In the middle of the 19th century, there was a house called Greenfield (previously called Retreat) beside the dispensary, which was occupied from about 1878 by the well-known dispensary doctor, Dr Albert Croly. When he married Miss C.E. Todd of Silveracres (Sarah Curran Avenue) in 1897, he moved to her house, where he died in 1934. He was also a Justice of the Peace (J.P.), and regularly "sat on the bench" in Rathfarnham Petty Sessions Court (District Court).

Mount Carmel Community Hospital, Braemor Park

In 1908, the Carmelite priests bought the house called Ardavon for use as a House of Study, which is reputed to have been built by Waldron in 1847 (Waldron's Bridge was nearby). The priests recorded that it was a farmhouse before they bought it, with a farmyard, a barn for 50 tons of hay, stables for three horses, accommodation for cows, coachman's house, fruit garden with three big glasshouses (two for growing peaches). The big room at the side of the house had been a ballroom. The priests remember that at the time of purchase, there was a small racecourse in the valley below the property, with two water jumps, which sounds like the site of the present hockey pitches of The High School. The novitiate moved to Terenure College from 1909 to 1917, and when they returned, they built the rear extensions, including the oratory, in 1922 and 1923, holding the "Pax Carnival" to raise funds. The property was re-named as Mount Carmel in 1937. They stayed until 1949, and then moved to the 50-acre Gort Muire in Ballinteer which they still occupy.

The Little Company of Mary, called the Blue Sisters because of their bright blue veil, bought the house in 1949, and opened Mount Carmel Hospital for 30 patients the following year. These nuns were founded in Nottingham, England, in 1877, by Mary Potter (now Venerable), and spread to Ireland in 1886, when they took over St John's Hospital in Limerick. They established the Milford Care Centre in Limerick in 1928 (now a Hospice), and in 1953 they also built a new hospital in Renmore, Galway.

In 1960 the nuns built the modern Mount Carmel Hospital in Dublin, and used the old house as their convent. The hospital was extended in 1969. Although well-known as a private Maternity Hospital, the nuns actually ran a General Hospital, with the whole range of medical services. Some local people will remember the small rear chapel (built by the Carmelites), which was open to the public for daily Mass.

The nuns sold the hospital to a developer in 2006 for €50 million, just before the "property crash", and it continued in operation until closure in 2014. Thankfully it was acquired by the HSE in 2015, and re-opened as the Mount Carmel Community Hospital, a "step-down" facility. The Blue Nuns built themselves a fine three-storey convent cum nursing home at the rear of the hospital site, beside the entrance to the Church of Ireland Theological College, and converted the original hospital domestic staff accommodation block into their own kitchens and offices. The old convent is now empty, and will probably be re-developed by the HSE. The odd bay window above the front porch had decorative stained glass, but this was removed and inserted into the hall doors of the new convent, providing a link with the past.

Church of Ireland Theological Institute, Braemor Park

Up on the hill overlooking The High School hockey pitches, stands a lovely red-bricked building, which was built as the Adelaide Convalescent Home in 1894, on a plot of land known as Newtown Cottage. The actual Adelaide Hospital was located on Peter Street (behind Jacobs Biscuit Factory), and was converted into apartments during the "celtic tiger" years (1995-2007), following the Hospitals amalgamation with Tallaght Hospital in 1998.

The convalescent home in Churchtown was loaned to the British War Department in 1915, for use as an Auxiliary Military Hospital, treating wounded soldiers shipped home from the Western Front, during the First World War, and became known as the Fetherstonhaugh Convalescent Home, even after it reverted to civilian use in 1919.

During the war, besides the men who enlisted in the British Army to fight, thousands of Irish civilians, mostly women, volunteered their services in temporary military hospitals, and making surgical dressings and clothes for the men on the Western Front. Those who were injured on the battlefield were sent back on Hospital Ships to England and Ireland to temporary hospitals, arriving at the North Wall Quay, transferred to Hospital Trains bound for Cork or Belfast, or transferred by the Royal Irish Automobile Club (RIAC) or St Johns Ambulance to various locations around Dublin. The military hospitals were manned by Army Doctors and Nurses, but assisted by Voluntary Aid Detachment (VAD) personnel, who had been trained by the British Red Cross and the St Johns Ambulance Brigade, and awarded First Aid Certificates.

In the early part of the War, the Fetherstonhaugh Auxiliary Hospital catered mainly for general surgical cases, but in the last eighteen months, functioned as an annexe to the Duke of Connaught Hospital in Bray, for the treatment and healing of stumps after amputation of limbs, in preparation for artificial limbs. During the hospitals four-year life in Braemor Park, 461 patients were treated, and only two died. The impressive hospital in Bray was originally the Meath Industrial School for Girls (an orphanage), and is nowadays the Loreto St Patricks National School, near the Town Hall. Artificial limbs were commercially made by Smith & Sheppard, but also at the Blackrock Orthopaedic Hospital on Carysfort Avenue, which was formerly the Meath Industrial School for Boys.

The Adelaide Convalescent Home was sold to the Representative Church Body (RCB) in 1961, and converted into a Divinity Hostel for seminarians studying in Trinity College Dublin. A large extension was added in 1964 for bedrooms. The RCB library/archives was built fronting on to Braemor Park in the late 1960's. The Hostel is now called the Church of Ireland Theological Institute.

St Luke's Hospital, Highfield Road

When Highfield Road (called the Old Rathgar Road up until the late 1860's) was laid out in the middle of the 18th century, Rathgar House was one of the first residences to be built, and its first occupier was the Wilson family. Within a few decades, the Farrans, who were solicitors, were in residence, and they stayed until 1853. The Todd family, part owners of Todd Burns department store in Mary Street in the city centre (now Penneys), demolished the old Rathgar House, and built Oaklands a little to the south of the original house around 1855. The Brown family, partners in the Brown Thomas department store in Grafton Street, enjoyed the property from 1865 to 1893, after which Charles Wisdom Hely took over.

The Hely family immediately formed an impressive secondary entrance to the site from Orwell Park, with granite pillars and ornamental wrought-iron gates incorporating the initials CWH. A charming red-brick gate lodge was built at the same time, but they still retained the gate lodge on Highfield Road. The family added a major extension to the north of the main house around 1912/1913, and the two impressive bow windows in the south elevation of the old house may have been added around this time as well.

Charles Bardon Healy founded the famous stationers and printers in Dame Street in 1848, and his son, Charles Wisdom, took over in 1886. Helys went public in 1896, at the same time as they took over the printers, Mecredy & Kyle, and the brand-new Acme Works in Dame Lane/Dame Court. Among his many interests, Charles Wisdom Hely was a director of the Dunlop Tyre Company in the early 20th century, and is reputed to have been an avid car buff – even the 1911 census refers to his Motor Houses (garages) in the grounds of Oaklands, by which time he describes his occupation as a Magistrate.

Part of the land alongside Highfield Road was sold to a developer for housing (Oakland Drive) in the late 1930's, and the impressive cast-iron gates, pillars, and curved railings moved to their current position.

The entire property was sold in 1950, and the lovely brochure prepared by the auctioneers, Good & Ganly, makes interesting reading. The two-storey over basement house had nine bedrooms, beautiful reception rooms, and numerous bedrooms for the servants. The sittingroom with one of the bow windows, had been painted by an Italian artist in 1895, and included silk tapestries on the walls. Most areas throughout the house had hardwood parquet flooring. Adjacent to the north-east of the house, there was a badminton hall, 120 feet by 50 feet, which was also used for private plays, concerts, and balls. The stables had been converted to apartments (flats) for the four gardeners. The three garages could hold fourteen cars. Besides ornamental trees and shrubs, there were two tennis courts, a croquet lawn, an old shell house, and a small thatched summerhouse with a fireplace.

The Cancer Association of Ireland (Comhlachas Ailse na hEireann) was set up in November 1949 as a voluntary body by the Minister for Health, Dr Noel Browne, and it purchased Oaklands, on a 13-acre site, the following year. The house was opened in May 1951 as a hostel for 40 mobile patients, who were receiving cancer treatment in various Dublin hospitals. Also in 1951, G & T Crampton Ltd were awarded the contract to build a new 127-bed cancer hospital, designed by Thomas Kennedy, which was part opened in 1952, and was completed in 1954, with the Hospital Trusts Fund (effectively the Government-run Irish Hospitals Horse-Racing Sweepstakes) providing the finance. The old house was converted at the same time to provide 33 beds, bringing the total capacity to 160-beds, both male and female. Various extensions, new buildings, and improvements, have been added over the last few decades, and the hospital is still going strong, under the recent control of the Health Service Executive (HSE).

The original 1855 house, Oakland, is now used as offices for the hospital management. The ground-floor Library still features wonderful ornate plasterwork and joinery, and the paintings on the ceiling and frieze, depicting tiny children (cherubs) at play, would not be out of place in a school or crèche. The nearby Boardroom is also spectacular, and still has the oak-block flooring. The other south room with a bow window, is also very attractive, although not as ornate as the library and boardroom.

The former detached Nurses Home (shaped like an H) at the south end of the leafy grounds, was converted in 1995 into a hostel for patients and families, and called Oakland Lodge.

Bloomfield Health Services
Bloomfield Hospital, specialising in mental health, was founded by Quakers in Bloomfield Avenue in Donnybrook in 1812, and moved to a brand-new hospital in Stocking Lane in 2005. The Quaker Archives is in a separate building at the entrance to the hospital campus, having originally occupied Swanbrook House beside the old hospital in Donnybrook.

"God's Acre", Whitechurch Road
Moravians are Protestant Christians, founded in the 15th century, in Moravia and Bohemia in the present Czech Republic, and spread to Ireland in the middle of the 18th century. After using various temporary churches, they built a church in 1755, set back from the street, at present-day 40 Lower Kevin Street. This was a simple rectangular building on an east-west axis, with four big round-headed windows in both the north and south elevations. In 1922, they built a wonderful granite-faced two-storey over basement Parochial Hall abutting Kevin Street, featuring a splendid hardwood double staircase, which acts as an archway leading to the courtyard and the church. There is one big room on the first floor, with a beautiful curved ceiling with wonderful cornices. The pediment at the top of the façade contains the emblem of the church, The Lamb of God, and the Latin words: "Vicit Agnus Noster eum Sequamur", which means, "Our Lamb Has Conquered, Let Us Follow Him." The church and hall closed in 1959, and the congregation ceased to practice in Ireland after 1980, but their Kevin Street premises has been beautifully restored and adapted to modern office and business use, with the former church accessed off the public side lane, and listed as 15a Bishop Street.

The Moravian cemetery in Rathfarnham, opposite the new Whitechurch Primary School, started on a half-acre site here in 1764, on the edge of the original Marlay demesne, and extended to one-acre in 1776. Their cemeteries are called "God's Acre".

Not unlike Quakers, they believe in the equality of all people, and hence they use small flat memorial stones on all graves, although, men and women are in separate sections. The Whitechurch cemetery is a lawn type, dotted with a few trees, with males on the right (looking in from the granite arched gateway), and females on the left, although a few modern graves near the gate do not fit this pattern. The rectangular granite slabs, size about 450mm wide and 600mm long, simply bear a name, date of birth, and date of death, with one person per grave. The inscription on the inside of the entrance arch reads: "THEM WHICH SLEEP IN JESUS WILL GOD BRING WITH HIM".

Dublin Society for Prevention of Cruelty to Animals (DSPCA)
This charity started in 1840 in the city centre, and in 1885 moved to Grand Canal Quay in Ringsend, and thereafter was fondly known as the Cats and Dogs Home. In 1990 they moved to Stocking Lane, and again in 2003 to their current purpose-built 32-acre campus on Mount Venus Road, which includes a veterinary hospital, dogs hotel, cats hotel, and charming open space and pond for the goats and geese.

Mount Carmel House of Studies in the days of the Carmelite fathers. The rear section was built by the priests. Note the viewing tower or belvedere, which was built in the second half of the 19th century by the Devine family. (Courtesy of Carmelite Library & Archives).

Mount Carmel Hospital convent now lies empty. Note the unusual additional bay window over the original porch.

Mount Carmel convent was extended to the rear by the Carmelite fathers in the early decades of the 20th century, and the belvedere tower demolished.

The former Adelaide Convalescent Home is now the Church of Ireland Theological Institute.

During the First World War, the Adelaide Convalescent Home was converted into the Fetherstonhaugh Military Hospital, managed by the Red Cross and Voluntary Aid Detachments (VAD). (Courtesy of National Library of Ireland).

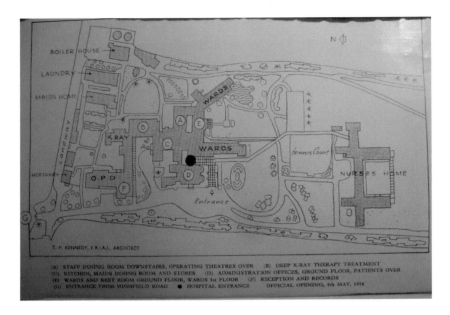

Layout plan of St Lukes Hospital in 1954. (Courtesy of National Library of Ireland).

Aerial view of St Lukes Hospital in 1954, with the Nurses Home in an H- block on the right. (Courtesy of National Library of Ireland).

The new St Lukes Hospital in 1954. (Courtesy of National Library of Ireland).

Rear of Oaklands in 1950 before it became St Lukes Hospital. The building on the right was the owner's private concert hall. (Courtesy of National Library of Ireland).

Private concert hall in Oaklands in 1950. (Courtesy of National Library of Ireland).

Oaklands in 1950 before it became St Lukes Hospital. (Courtesy of National Library of Ireland).

1950 view of one of the reception rooms in Oaklands, before it became St Lukes Hospital. (Courtesy of National Library of Ireland).

One of the former reception rooms in Oaklands is now the Library in St Lukes Hospital, with fabulous ceiling, cornices, etc.

Selected Sources

.

"Rathfarnham Roads", by Patrick Healy, 2005.

"A Portrait of St Columba's College, 1843-2013", by Patrick Wyse Jackson and Ninian Falkiner, 2013.

"Golf in the Foothills – A History of Grange Golf Club, 1919 – 2010", by Brian Treston and Michael Forde.

"Our Golfing Demesne: Castle Golf Club, 1913-2013".

"Rebellion & Revolution in Dublin: voices from a suburb, Rathfarnham, 1913-23", edited by Marnie Hay and Daire Keogh, 2016.

"The Rivers of Dublin", by Clair L. Sweeney, 1991.

"The Rivers Dodder & Poddle: Mills, Storms, Droughts, and the Public Water Supply", by Don McEntee & Michael Corcoran, 2016.

"Down the Dodder: wildlife, history, legend, walks", by Christopher Moriarty.

"Looking Forward – Looking Back, 50 Years of Scouting in Rathfarnham", 1992.

"John Philpot Curran: His Life and Times", by Leslie Hale, 1958.

"The Lilac Years", by Hilary McDonagh & Orla McKeown, 2000.

"Hallowed Fire", historic short documentary film on Evie Hone by Department of Foreign Affairs, 1950. Can be viewed on the Irish Film Institute iPlayer.

"Republican Loans", historic short documentary film about Michael Collins, selling Bonds at the Emmet Block, outside the entrance door of St Endas College, 1919. Can be viewed on Irish Film Institute iPlayer.

"The Topographical Dictionary of Ireland", by Samuel Lewis, 1837.

"Through Street Broad and Narrow – A History of Dublin Trams", by Michael Corcoran, 2008.

"Footprints of Emmet", by J.J. Reynolds, 1903.

"Celebrating 190 Years of Whitechurch Parish Rathfarnham", by Daphne Harkin, 2017.

"Hampshire and The Company of White Paper Makers", by J.H. Thomas.

"A Survey of the Lands of Rathfarnham belonging to the General Fund of the Protestant Dissenters", by John Byrne, 1801.

"Map of Rathfarnham Park", Richard Frizell, 1779.

"Deanery of Taney" manuscript, by Rev. Myles V. Ronan.

"Records & Recollections: A History of the Diocesan Secondary School for Girls, 1849-1974", by Muriel Jogoe & Enid Oldham, 1986.

"Faithful to our Trust: A History of the Erasmus Smith Trust, and The High School Dublin", by W.J.R. Wallace, 2004.

Souvenir Brochure, 1954, for the opening of St Luke's Hospital.

"Statistical Survey of County Dublin", by Joseph Archer, 1801.

Other books by the same author

"Harold's Cross", The History Press, 2011.

"Harold's Cross: A History", The History Press, 2016.

"Terenure", The History Press, 2014.

"Mount Merrion", The History Press, 2012.

"Blackrock", The History Press, 2014.

"Dundrum", The History Press, 2016.

"Ringsend", The History Press, 2017.

"Castlebar", The History Press, 2013.

"Drogheda", The History Press, 2013.

"Irish Temperance Halls", First Return Press, 2018.

"Times, Chimes & Charms of Dublin", First Return Press, 2012.

"Selected Churches of Dublin", First Return Press, 2012.

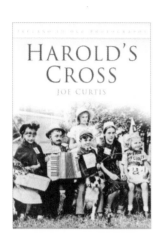

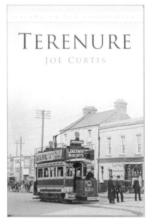

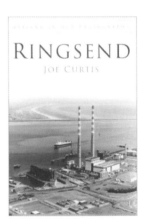

39147643R00098

Printed in Poland
by Amazon Fulfillment
Poland Sp. z o.o., Wrocław